IDEAS FOR GREAT

Home Decorating

By the editors of Sunset Books

SUNSET PUBLISHING CORP. • MENLO PARK, CA

SUNSET BOOKS

VP, Sales & Marketing: Richard A. Smeby
VP, Editorial Director: Bob Doyle
Production Director: Lory Day
Art Director: Vasken Guiragossian

IDEAS FOR GREAT HOME DECORATING was produced
in conjunction with Roundtable Press, Inc.
Directors: Marsha Melnick, Susan E. Meyer
Senior Editor: Carol Spier
Book Design: BTD/Beth Tondreau

STAFF FOR THIS BOOK:
Developmental Editor: Linda J. Selden
Research Consultants: Scott Atkinson, Christine Barnes
Principal Photographer: Philip Harvey
Photo Director: JoAnn Masaoka Van Atta
Illustrations: Susan Jaekel, Bill Oetinger, Mark Pechenik
Production Coordinator: Patricia S. Williams

6 7 8 9 10 11 12 13 14 15 16 17 18 19 QPD QPD 02 01 00

ISBN 0-376-01257-9
Library of Congress Catalog Card Number: 96-067823
Printed in the United States.

For additional copies of *Ideas for Great Home Decorating* or any other *Sunset* book,
call 1-800-526-5111, or see our website at: www.sunsetbooks.com

ON THE COVER:
*Pale painted stripes form a simple backdrop in a peaceful country bedroom; interior design
and photography by* David Duncan Livingston. *Cover design by* Vasken Guiragossian.
All other cover photography by Philip Harvey.

Foreword

W hen you decide to decorate or redecorate your home, you set forth on a quest to create your perfect environment. Some homeowners are blessed with a clear vision and are confident about the undertaking, while others find the redecorating prospect more daunting. Whether you consider the process exciting or intimidating you should embark on it as on any other adventure—dream first, consider your options and plan your route, and then set forth with a good itinerary that allows a few side trips—and a budget that has room for the unexpected.

Ideas for Great Home Decorating will guide you along your decorating journey. It begins with a brief introduction to style, which will help you choose and define the decor of your dreams. Part Two is devoted to design, providing a thorough overview of the principles and vocabulary of color and design, and presenting hundreds of options for incorporating, designing, or decorating the elements common to all rooms—windows and doors, wall coverings, window treatments, and flooring. Part Three takes you on a room-by-room tour,

offering hundreds of terrific ideas for making each part of your living space look great and work well. And an invaluable planning primer discusses the nitty-gritty of planning your decorating project so that it can be executed with ease.

Throughout the book you'll find some special features. Dozens of Great Ideas present wonderful details that add polish, finesse, or fun to a room—they'll encourage you to be creative and go beyond the obvious. And the many Facts & Tips include goal-defining questionnaires and provide important technical information— they'll help you make smart decisions.

So browse through the hundreds of inspiring photos, pick and choose among the clever concepts and smart solutions used by other homeowners, and be creative— adapt as many of these great ideas as suit your needs.

Contents

PART 1

Style

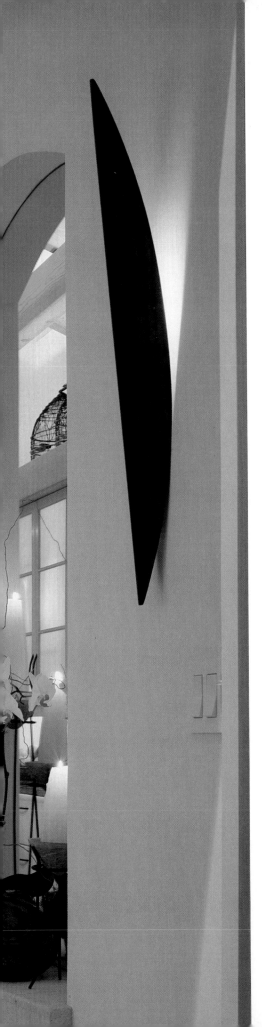

Introduction to Style

I n design, the word style has two meanings. Sometimes it refers to a "look" that can be defined by specific characteristics—each period, region, or artistic school has distinctive traits. But when we describe a design as "having great style" or being "stylish" we mean something else—we refer to the successful and possibly unique way in which the elements of the design are assembled, and the pleasure we derive from it.

You may want to choose a particular style when you undertake a decorating project. You will certainly strive to create a stylish decor.

As you look through this book, you will see many well-designed rooms. You will see many valid decorating approaches that may or may not appeal to you. Bear in mind that a design idea—a concept for how to solve a problem—can be interpreted in many styles. So if you see something you like, ask yourself what draws you to it, and whether it will look stylish in your home.

Soaring proportions and striking but simple architectural lines give this home an inherent contemporary style—and make it inherently stylish. The glass roof ridge dominates the space. White walls, stone flooring, and natural wood are the perfect foil for rattan, baskets, and wrought iron accessories. The effect is impressive, but calm and inviting.

STYLE AND MOOD

CONCENTRATE FOR THE MOMENT on choosing the style and mood of your dream decor. What is the difference? A style has physical characteristics that identify it with a particular region, era, or artistic movement—Victorian, Southwestern, Arts and Crafts. A mood is the ambience that develops when a style is interpreted—cozy, inviting, serene. What matters is that you choose a style and mood you find attractive and comfortable.

Opposite: While one would be hard pressed to label the style of this room as anything more specific than "eclectic period," there is no question that style it has, indeed. It is gracious and comfortable; the furnishings are well-proportioned; the mood is intriguing; and it indicates an owner with diverse interests. Although there is a lot going on, the pattern scales are balanced and the limited palette unifies and controls the many elements.

Right: Quiet, serene, and restful, this contemporary room could not be more different from the one opposite. It is as spare and simple as can be, with clean architectural lines and minimal trim. The neutral color scheme plays up the beauty of the woodwork. A mirrored partition expands the space, showcases an equally spare yet beautiful planter, and plays a gentle trick on the eye.

PERIOD STYLE

OLD AND REPRODUCTION HOMES often are decorated in a style that suits their architecture. While some owners are meticulous in assembling "period" furnishings of a specific historic style, many choose traditional pieces with a variety of characteristic shapes to create a look that is generally evocative of past eras. Whether your period style is museumlike or just graciously traditional, include pieces that can take everyday use.

Raised panel cherry cabinetry gives this kitchen a traditional look sometimes referred to as Early American. Of course, early American kitchens did not have today's features, and raised panel doors are not unique to America—but the effect is appropriate for a traditional home. If these cabinets were painted or distressed, the mood would change.

Opposite: The style is loosely Neoclassical and definitely formal in this elegantly proportioned room, where antique and new furnishings mix easily together. Furniture lines are graceful and delicate, and seem doubly so in such a grand room. Paneled walls are softened by a draped window treatment that carries the eye upward with a great flourish.

REGIONAL STYLE

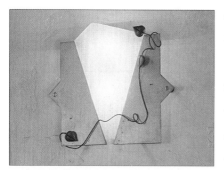

AROUND THE GLOBE, climate and available resources have mixed with cultural sensibilities to create unique styles of architecture and furnishings. One of these styles may appeal to you for cultural, aesthetic, or sentimental reasons, or you may live where a particular style is indigenous. Even if your architecture does not support your chosen style, you can use color, fabric, wallcovering, and other furnishings to recreate its ambience.

Sliding shoji screens send a soft light over the dark wood furniture and Oriental accessories in this small dining room, creating an impression of Japanese style—though this Western table and chairs would not be found in a Japanese home. Still, the room has the careful composition of a Japanese print, and a wonderful serene ambience.

Below: A white plastered fireplace with a terra-cotta hearth is the cornerstone of this Southwest-inspired decor. The all-white room with its built-in banquette, trimless windows, and exposed ceiling beams has the feeling of an adobe dwelling. Native American pottery, baskets, and patterned textiles complete the look.

Call this wine-country style, or contemporary Mediterranean, as you will. Saturated colors and decorative painting set the mood, which is sun-drenched and warm.

The mirror reflects a nearby garden, making this tiny breakfast nook feel larger. Custom sconces give a witty twist to the decor, and provide needed light.

ROMANTIC STYLE

STRICTLY SPEAKING, ROMANTIC ISN'T A STYLE, but an intimate mood created by draped fabrics, florals, lace, and nostalgic accessories. Victorian decors are often romantic, but those of many other periods may be as well. The current vogue for fanciful canopy beds with gauzy draperies is surely romantic. Usually pretty and feminine, the true hallmarks of romantic are, not surprisingly, very subjective. Here are a few options.

Sunlight washes over the old-fashioned claw-foot tub set at an angle in this eclectic bathing area, which seems to be more of a boudoir than a bathroom—and if a boudoir is not romantic, what is? Pale yellow walls and sheer drapery make a soft backdrop for the fern, big bouquet of roses, and tub with elegant brass fittings.

Opposite above: The delicate frills and flourishes in this room evoke an era of fairy-tale romance—perhaps a little girl's dreams come true. The charming wallpainting sets the mood. The furniture seems brushed with gold, and the accessories are sweetly nostalgic for yesteryear. Note how perfectly the chintz on the diminutive chairs complements the mural.

Opposite below: This bedroom is traditionally furnished. The elaborate formal window and bed draperies set up an intimate mood that is enhanced by the floral print, shirred welting, and lush tasseled fringe. The white bed linens have a pretty lace edging. The scalloped valance, gathered bed skirt, plump pillows, and puffed comforter all contribute to the romantic mood.

COUNTRY STYLE

COUNTRY DECOR HAS two principal demeanors. To some, country is rustic, distressed, or quaint—with stenciled walls, American quilts, and lots of checks. To others it is simple, spare, and filled with fresh air—with Shaker-style furnishings and minimal but distinctive accessories. The difference is really one of degree—both favor the handcrafted over the factory-made. Country decor can be eclectic, formal, or casual.

Pale blue stripes form a simple backdrop in this peaceful country bedroom. The black steel canopy bed is new, handmade, and unadorned with curtains. The other furniture is old, though the accessories are not. A lace shade dapples the wall with roses. Note how the painted picture rail raises the ceiling and ties in nicely with the bed frame. (See pages 6–7 for a larger view of this room.)

Right: Perhaps because they are so fresh, blue and white are traditional country colors. This kitchen-dining area gets a nineteenth-century farmhouse ambience from the high wainscoted walls, window seat, and pendant lamp; the floral tiles, topiaries, and plates on the wall add a dressy twist.

Below: Folk art and collectibles are an important part of many country decors. This corner celebrates both with a collection of trompe l'oeil and real objects mingling playfully on a picture-rail shelf. Only the candle sconce, birdcage and doll are real—the rest are painted in place. Glazed walls add a sunny glow and checked Roman shades give a tailored, unfussy finish to the French doors.

CONTEMPORARY STYLE

NEW AND EXCITING IDEAS for home design make the most of new materials and technologies to bring light, air, and convenience into our lives. Contemporary design tends to be sleek, strong, and graphic, with bold colors and shapes set against plain backgrounds. Contemporary style makes a natural showcase for artwork or outstanding furniture. If you mix in a little old with the new, the hard-edged effect will be softened.

While open-plan living puts the kitchen at the heart of the home, contemporary kitchens are anything but cozy and quaint. This one features simple, elegant cabinetry, perhaps inspired by the recent appreciation for Shaker design, and looks sophisticated when viewed from adjacent living areas. Note the juxtaposition of sleek materials and twig sculpture.

Opposite: Contemporary celebrates the new, yet often pays homage to the recent past that paved the way for current trends. Witness this retro-fifties great room, where rich pastels set the tone and divide the living areas. Shapes are streamlined, but a little plump—like cars of that era. Fluorescent kitchen lighting, required by some building codes, works perfectly here.

Rather than hiding structural and finishing materials, contemporary design sometimes shows them off. This glass counter and basin are elegant, sophisticated, and totally functional. The spare, wall-mounted fittings—and any water leaving the tap—are reflected in the mirror with sculptural finesse. Wide drawers enhance the stream-lined look of the cabinet.

Glass is a featured component in many contemporary homes. This two-story sunroom makes a dramatic link for living and sleeping areas; the balcony hallway is blessed with touch-the-sky and garden views. When the glass doors are wide open, the flagstone floor flows seamlessly to the terrace. Be aware that glass rooms may require special climate control.

As the world becomes smaller, we gain a new appreciation for design from different regions inspired by different cultures—and we adapt it to our own homes. Here a Japanese-style dining area opens off a two-story living room. The transition from leather sofas to platform seating seems perfectly natural—the clean, graphic lines of the architecture complement both styles.

Color, Pattern, and Design Principles

*G*ood design doesn't just happen, except in nature. Instead, design involves a conscious, subjective process of selecting and organizing materials and objects in a visually pleasing way. When well executed, good design is as functional and comfortable as it is beautiful. But design is not just the province of interior designers and architects. Every time you choose a paint color or arrange furniture in a room, you are making design decisions.

While there are basic guidelines for your design decisions, the most important tool you have is your eyes. Be observant, have opinions, learn to recognize things that please you, and analyze why. And be a collector—don't hesitate to clip magazines, get swatches, or even to save beautiful pebbles. Then test samples in your room, get help if you need it, and trust your instincts.

Deep, rich, saturated color on a wall is always a surprise—when you walk into a room like this you catch your breath. These dark rose walls are glazed, so they glow with an extra sheen in the lamplight. Deep-color walls lend an elegant finish to a decor, and will intensify the mood.

ALL ABOUT COLOR

BECAUSE COLOR MAKES SUCH AN EMOTIONAL contribution to design, it is possibly the first thing you think about when you are decorating. Even if you feel insecure about working with color, you are sure to recognize combinations and effects that please you. To develop confidence, look for examples of color palettes in all sorts of places—clothing, automobiles, wrapping paper. Nature and art are great teachers, too.

A saturated palette sets the striking tone in this room, and painted paneling provides a beginning point for the design. The brightly accented molding creates a pattern on the dark wall that serves as built-in frames for windows, wallpaintings, and the faux-stone panel. Rich colors move in and out of the furnishings, contrasted always by the ecru in the fabric and checkerboard floor.

This rustic kitchen also has an ecru, green, russet, and black decor, but the intensity and balance are completely different from the room opposite. The tones are softer, the green has become verdigris, and the ecru is sponged with amber; they are of equal weight in the design. Russet and soft black accents are found in the plaid, the flowers, the wrought iron table base, and the sink counter.

Deep, rich, bright yellow is the color of sunshine, marigolds, and here—happiness. Ceiling, walls, and window treatments positively radiate, while the worn blue cupboard offers a muted contrast that quiets them down. Note how a whole rainbow of rich hues trims the cradle; when a primary color dominates, stay away from flimsy pastel accents.

Opulent furnishings demand a dramatic background. Here uneven plaster walls were rag-rolled with vivid red and varnished to resemble leather. The room is filled with curiosities, and the effect is mysterious, like an exotic wood box filled with sparkling jewels and ivory. Imagine the same items against a white wall—they would be lovely, but some of their magic would be gone.

A black-and-white scheme is sharp and clean. It can accent or be accented by any other color for a forceful graphic effect. In this eclectic-Oriental-style dining area, red walls stand up handsomely to the black-and-white table setting. White ceiling and window casings reiterate the contrast.

Above right: We sometimes forget that appliances have color—and we don't always have a lot of choice about it. This kitchen makes a virtue out of a stainless refrigerator with glass doors. The taupe woodwork trimming the mustard walls gives a sophisticated touch to the country room, and niche cabinets make a home for the refrigerator, melding tones effortlessly.

UNDERSTANDING COLOR

COLOR VOCABULARY

To understand and use color theory, you need to know some basic terms and concepts.

Hue

Hue is just another word for color. Royal blue, fire engine red, and bright yellow are hues, as are such softer colors as dove gray, terracotta, and cream.

• Each hue has a visual "temperature." Yellow, orange, and red are warm and lively; they're often referred to as advancing colors because they seem nearer than they actually are. Blue, green, and violet are cool and tranquil; they're called receding colors because they appear farther away than they actually are.

Value

Value refers to the lightness or darkness of color.

• The more white in a color, the lighter the value; these colors, called tints, lie just inside the hue ring on the color wheel (opposite, near left).

• The more black in a color, the darker the color's value; these colors, termed shades, appear just outside the hue ring on the color wheel.

• Color with gray added is a tone.

• Adding white, black, or gray to colors to make tints, shades, or tones is called extending colors.

Intensity

This is the degree of purity, or saturation, of color. Although both pale pink and bright red are technically red, they differ in their intensity, or strength, of color. You increase a color's intensity by adding more of the pure color; adding white, black, or the color's complement (opposite, left) reduces intensity. Full-intensity colors are so strong and stimulating that they're usually used only for emphasis in decorating.

THE COLOR WHEEL

As you look at the color wheel, keep in mind that its colors are almost always altered and combined in ways that soften their impact. All color combinations, from safe to audacious, come from variations and combinations on the basic color wheel. Although the color wheel can't dictate formula schemes, it can help you imagine what will happen when colors are put together. And, if you have a definite color in mind, the color wheel expands your choices by allowing you to build a number of different schemes.

Primary colors

Red, blue, and yellow are the primary colors; they are the source of all other colors. Primaries are powerful, usually too powerful to use at full strength on large expanses, such as walls.

Secondary colors

When equal parts of two primary colors are combined, secondary colors are formed: green comes from blue and yellow, orange from yellow and red, and violet from red and blue. Secondary colors lie midway between the primary colors on the color wheel; they are less strong than primaries.

Intermediate colors

When a primary color is mixed with an adjacent secondary color, an intermediate color is formed: blue (a primary) and violet (a secondary) combine to make blue-violet, an intermediate.

Tertiary and quaternary colors

Subtle blends of pure color, tertiary and quaternary colors are richer hues than shades, which are made by adding black.

• Tertiary colors are formed when two secondary colors are mixed. They add depth and sophistication to a color scheme. Look at the color circle (opposite, right) and follow the arrows to make the tertiaries: green and orange make wheat; orange and violet make brick; and violet and green make slate. Note that the tertiaries shown have had varying amounts of white added to them.

• Quaternary colors are formed when two tertiary colors are mixed: wheat and brick become sandstone, brick and slate become eggplant, and slate and wheat become juniper.

Complementary colors

Colors that lie opposite each other on the color wheel are known as complementary colors. Red and green are complements, as are blue and orange, yellow and violet. Complementary colors are stimulating and full of surprises.

- Used in their full intensity, they seem harsh. When mixed in equal amounts, they neutralize each other, forming a flat, neutral gray.
- When a small amount of one color is added to its complement, the result is a pleasing, less intense version of the predominant color. The inner wedges on the color wheel (below, left) show tints that have a bit of complement added, forming extended and neutralized colors.

COLOR CHARACTERISTICS

Colors have qualities that can work magic on walls. Understanding the characteristics of color will open up a world of design ideas and make it easier for you to choose the right paint or wall-covering color for your room.

How light affects color

The quality of light, whether natural or artificial, can greatly affect colors. That is why it's so important to examine a large sample of the color you think you want under different light conditions.

- Cool fluorescent light amplifies cool colors and weakens warm ones: under cool light, a blue-base color seems more blue, but a yellow-base color appears duller. Warm incandescent light enhances warm colors while weakening cool ones.
- Reflected light behaves in much the same way. Light bouncing off a cool green lawn into a room, for example, will have a different effect than light reflecting off a warm brick wall. Light tinted with a certain color will raise the intensity of similar colors and neutralize complementary colors.
- Light also alters a color's value. Low light darkens value and reduces intensity; a higher light level lightens value and increases intensity. Too much light can make colors look washed out.

ALTERING SPACE WITH COLOR

A color's visual temperature can alter the sense of space in a room.
- Warm colors such as apricot, yellow, and terra-cotta appear to advance. Walls finished in those colors seem closer, making the room appear smaller. You can easily take advantage of this to make a large room feel more intimate.
- Blue, green, and violet, on the other hand, are cool, serene hues that seem to recede. Walls painted these colors tend to make a room appear more spacious than it really is.
- Intensity and value also play a role in altering the perception of room size. More intense colors make a room seem smaller, while low-intensity colors visually increase the sense of space. Darker values (shades) diminish room size because they absorb light. Unbroken expanses of very light values reflect the light and open up space.
- Whatever the colors, intensities, or values, a great deal of contrast has the same impact as a dark color—it reduces the perceived space. Conversely, harmonious monochromatic and analogous schemes have the tendency to enlarge space. Neutrals of similar value also seem to make the walls retreat, allowing the emphasis to fall on furnishings.

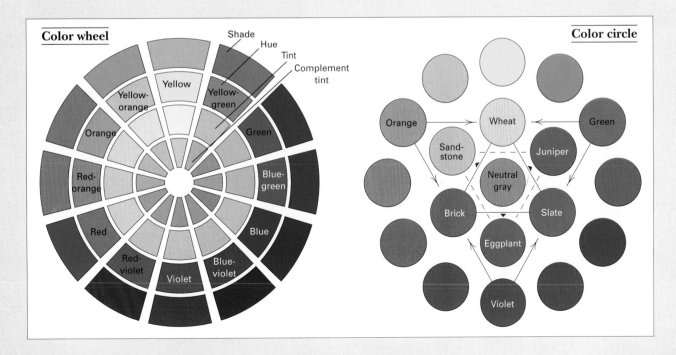

In an all-white room, architecture and furnishings blend and become sculptural studies in which light and shadow are of primary importance. Here a soaring ceiling dwarfs the room; skylights throw planes and angles into relief; and windows dominate and punctuate the walls. The views are like paintings. Contemporary architecture and all-white schemes are natural mates.

Pale walls, white walls, creamy walls—all maximize the effects of natural or artificial light to make a room seem spacious, airy, and bright. A light neutral background gives you the freedom to focus your design with the color of your furnishings—by choosing any color you like. Here rose-colored furnishings take center stage against a creamy background. The ecru pattern adds life. Natural wood and glass add gentle accents.

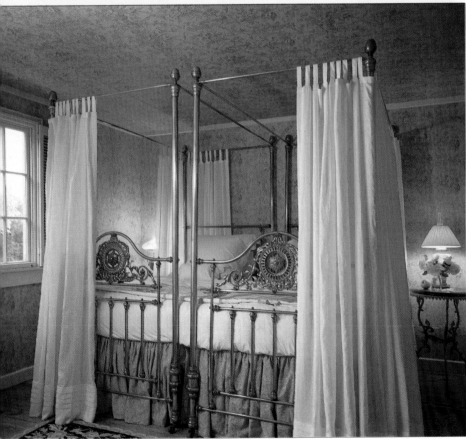

Monochromatic and tone-on-tone color schemes are restful and soothing—with one caveat: Too much of a dark or bright color can be oppressive; all colors appear to increase in intensity as they increase in volume. Here an all-over pattern of rose and taupe on pale pink creates a peach background. The brass beds and wood floor blend with it, while cream linens contrast and absorb it.

HAVING FUN WITH COLOR

THE EFFECT OF COLOR on a room comes not only from the palette that you select, but also from the way you use the various hues. You need not rely on printed patterns to convey character—you can use color to highlight or contrast your architecture, use fields of solid color to create a pattern, pick an unusual palette, even paint a subtle multihued surface. Here are some ideas that depend upon wit.

An unusual palette will make you sit up and take notice. Sponged, intensely peach walls give a wry acknowledgment to the cavelike atmosphere of this basement office, which began life as a closet. Purple and lavender trim draw your eyes to the windows. This color combination is a little out of the ordinary, yet no less pleasing for being unexpected.

Opposite: This home office is a canvas on which solid color makes a witty abstract painting. Fields of color emphasize—and break up—the natural planes of the architecture. Horizontal bands of molding divide fields of color. Zigzags and curves make geometric transitions where you least expect to find them. Even the window valance has a witty edge.

While not at all fancy, this room is far from ho-hum. Carefully placed color highlights the many interesting architectural details—natural warm tones of wood are built into the floor, column, beams, and rafters. Cool blues give importance to the cupboard, bench, and window sash. Rust mullions give an unexpected graphic finish to the window and echo the door.

COLOR SCHEMES

COLOR COMBINATIONS

Once you see how the different color combinations are formed, you can build your own combinations from a favorite color or colors. Even if the color combination you have in mind doesn't fit any of the schemes described, it can still be a smashing success.

• You don't have to think of colors in their full intensities. By neutralizing (adding a bit of a color's complement) and extending (adding white, black, or gray) them, you'll change the character of colors and form more sophisticated combinations.

Monochromatic

Monochromatic schemes—combinations that employ one color in a variety of intensities and values—are simple to put together and easy to live with because they're so restful. Since colors have so much in common in monochromatic schemes, rooms appear unified and harmonious. Contrasting values will create interest, but too much variation may look uneven.

Complementary

Based on any two colors opposite each other on the color wheel, complementary schemes are richer than monochromatic ones because they balance warm and cool colors (see drawing below). Depending upon the hues, these combinations can be startling or subdued. Look beyond such obviously jarring complements as intense yellow and violet to see the possibilities of quiet combinations, such as cream and amethyst (tints of yellow and violet, each slightly neutralized).

• A triad combination consists of any three colors equidistant from each other on the color wheel.

• A split complement also contains three colors—one primary or intermediate color plus the color on each side of its opposite. Yellow plus red-violet and blue-violet is one example of a split complement.

• A double split complement comes from splitting both sides of the color wheel, resulting in a four-color scheme.

Analogous

Varied yet harmonious, analogous, or related, color combinations are composed of two or more colors that lie next to each other on the color wheel. The most agreeable analogous combinations are limited to colors falling between two primaries and including one of those primaries—yellow-green, green, blue-green, and blue for example. Note that every hue contains at least a touch of the primary color.

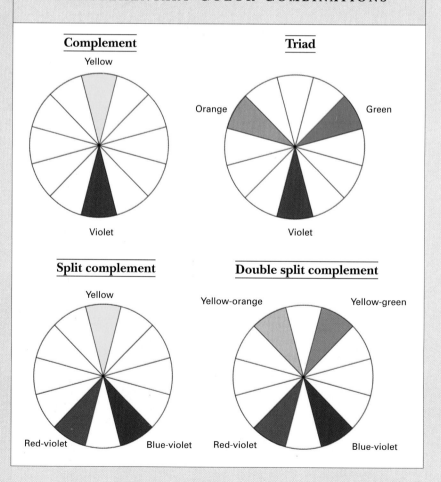

COMPLEMENTARY COLOR COMBINATIONS

Complement
Yellow
Violet

Triad
Orange
Green
Violet

Split complement
Yellow
Red-violet
Blue-violet

Double split complement
Yellow-orange
Yellow-green
Red-violet
Blue-violet

EXAMPLES OF COLOR SCHEMES

Shown *(clockwise from upper left)* are four color schemes, each based around a different print fabric. • A triad of quaternaries—sandstone, eggplant, and juniper—plus a tint of violet combine in a jungle pattern. • An analogous combination of blue and green tints, shades, and tones is warmed by peach, blue's complement. • High-intensity hues from all around the color wheel produce a bold, balanced scheme softened by. less-intense peach. • This impressionistic pattern is composed of primaries and secondaries that are similar in value and intensity.

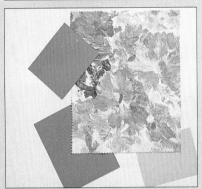
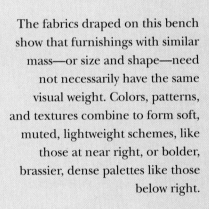

The fabrics draped on this bench show that furnishings with similar mass—or size and shape—need not necessarily have the same visual weight. Colors, patterns, and textures combine to form soft, muted, lightweight schemes, like those at near right, or bolder, brassier, dense palettes like those below right.

THE DESIGN PROCESS

DURING THE PROCESS OF DESIGNING a room, there are specific elements with which designers work, and principles that they observe in arranging them. If you think of *color, space, line, texture,* and *pattern* as the designer's raw materials, and consider the principles of *balance, scale, emphasis, rhythm,* and *harmony* as the tools by which these materials are arranged, you will begin to understand how designers achieve pleasing effects.

Because motifs have connotations that affect the way we perceive them, pattern adds unique character to a decor. Pattern also adds variation to a color scheme, and sometimes texture. Here a fabric panel accents the architectural detail of the room; its tone-on-tone coloration adds texture and echoes the walls and trim.

The elements of design work to perfection in this room. The cream, green, and peach *color* scheme is pleasing; the design *lines* are stately but not static; the textiles add soft and shimmery *textures;* the subtle use of *pattern* adds unexpected punctuation to the *rhythm* of the arrangement; the *scale* of the furnishings is *balanced*—and the overall effect is *harmonious.*

Opposite: Strong horizontal and vertical lines dominate this imposing interior. Each surface is broken with rectilinear planes—square-edged pilasters wrapped with flat capitals, dropped ceiling with recessed skylight, the leading in the windows. Oxidized copper and beveled glass add texture and give a cool cast to the buff walls, ceiling, and floor.

ABOUT DESIGN

An understanding of basic design elements and principles will help you start the design process. Although the concepts may seem abstract, they need to be considered and applied as you develop your own style.

ELEMENTS OF DESIGN

Color may be first and foremost among the design elements, but space, line, texture, and pattern are also critical to a decorating scheme. As you consider the many choices for furnishings, keep those elements in mind. A successful mix will help you achieve a balanced, beautiful room.

Space

Walls enclose and define the space called a room. How space is perceived depends on the way color, line, texture, and pattern are used on and inside the walls.

- To make a small room seem larger, emphasize openings to let the eye travel to the space beyond. Use small to medium-size textures and patterns on walls. Employ light, cool colors on walls and ceilings.
- To make a large room seem smaller, use a contrasting color, texture, or pattern to define or create distinct areas. Use dark, warm colors on walls and ceilings. Introduce rough textures such as combed plaster on walls to advance them visually.

Line

The "lines" of a room refer to the room's shape or the dominant visual direction created by all the decorating elements. A room can incorporate many different lines—vertical, horizontal, diagonal, angular, and curved. Directional patterns on wallcoverings, decorative moldings, and window treatments can alter your perception of a room's size.

Texture

Rough plaster, velvet, the softness of drapery, and the sheen of marble or glossy paint are a few examples of texture. Patterns on fabric and special paint techniques such as sponging possess a visual texture. Whether tactile or visual, texture adds interest to a decor, and can make it feel warmer or cooler. Texture tends to fill space and can make a room seem smaller or cozier.

Pattern

Pattern brings rhythm and vitality to a room, unifying colors and textures with design. Thinking about how patterns appear on walls and how they interact will make the job of choosing and combining patterns easier.

- Naturalistic patterns are realistic renderings of natural forms, such as flowers. Stylized patterns simplify natural designs to capture their essence; the fleur-de-lis, a stylized iris, is an example. Geometric designs such as plaids and checks are nonrepresentational. Abstract patterns are loose, artistic interpretations of realistic or geometric designs.
- The size of a design motif when seen in relation to other motifs is referred to as scale. Some small-scale patterns are so small that they read like a textured surface. To keep a room from appearing too small, choose a pattern with an open, airy background; your eye will look through the pattern and beyond, making the room seem more spacious. A generously proportioned room will support large, brightly colored motifs, even when they appear on dark backgrounds. Because they have the effect of drawing the walls closer, large patterns can consume space and create the impression that the room is smaller than it actually is.

PRINCIPLES OF DESIGN

Although these basic principles deal with intangibles, they're very important for establishing a successful decor.

Balance

When a sense of visual equilibrium is achieved in a room, the design is balanced. To achieve balance, you need to think about the visual weight of the elements. Balance in a room may be symmetrical or asymmetrical. Few rooms are completely symmetrical, but there are often symmetrical elements, such as a centered fireplace or identical chairs facing each other.

Rhythm

The organized repetition of elements in a design scheme constitutes rhythm. This repetition brings a sense of unity and continuity as your eye moves easily from one motif or area to another. While the repeated elements must share a common trait, such as color, for a sense of unity, they should also be varied to create visual interest.

Emphasis

Emphasis suggests making some elements in a design more significant than others. If a work of art is the focal point in a room, for example, the furnishings and wall coverings should be subordinate. Without emphasis, a room looks monotonous.

Scale

When the scale of a wall covering, for example, is in proportion to the overall size of the room, the room appears harmonious. If the scale is too large for the room, the effect will be overpowering; if it's too small, the design will look flimsy or weak.

Harmony

When both unity and variety exist in a room, harmony results. A careful combining of colors, textures, and patterns produces a unified whole. Too much unity, however, can be boring. Variety—in just the right amount—contributes vitality and excitement to a room's design. It may be subtle, as in slight color variations, or it may be startling, as with sharply contrasting patterns.

Top: Texture and pattern are not always added during the decorating process; sometimes they are part of the architecture. If so, you may want to acknowledge them and allow them to set the tone. Here a stone wall dominates the decor, which is otherwise quite stark. The soft pattern on the daybed is a subtle complement to the stone.

Bottom: Exposed structural beams silhouetted against this vaulted ceiling create a strong pattern that is balanced by the freestanding plastered fireplace. The room is devoid of trim, so the windows and clerestory niches add simple graphic accents. Stripes on the desk wall add another linear motif. The furnishings provide a soft, muted contrast.

Above left: Bold patterns can be mixed successfully if they have a common palette and the scale of their motifs is balanced. Here the wallpaper sets the pace. The window shade repeats its colors in a stripe while the curtain sends up faint echoes. The floor and table drape offer a sober contrast.

Above right: One rule of thumb for mixing patterns is to include motifs in three scales. This assures that the over-all effect will be rhythmic, and that the eye will be drawn to different furnishings. Here a large floral stripe tops the bed, a mid-size one covers walls and ceiling, and a small allover floral lines the dormer. The print on the shade is so small it becomes a solid color.

Left: The monumental proportions of this bed assure that it dominates the decor, but its imposing effect is softened by the generous comforter and fabric in the ceiling bays (note how the color in the positive-negative pattern is reversed). The oversize pots are well-proportioned for this space.

This bathroom is full of unexpected curves and angles that move rhythmically—and rather wittily—along the wall. The curlicues and scallops seem to ebb and flow like a wave. The only surface patterns come from the veining of the marble, and small black squares in the floor echoed by the regular repeat of tiles set in relief on the wall.

USING BORDERS

Adding a border to a wall can magically transform a room. You can use borders to highlight architectural details or to give the effect of trim where none exists. There are hundreds of wallpaper and fabric borders to choose from. You can also paint one using stencils.

Coordinated fabrics and wallpapers make it possible to create a foolproof unified look. Here a wallpaper border divides upper and lower walls; a strip of fabric makes another border on the valance.

Custom border designs require careful planning and attention to detail. Here a gold rococo border features square cutouts at the corners; the floral spray adds an unexpected flourish.

Why not apply multiple adjoining borders to create a strong decorative accent? These richly ornamented borders capture the spirit of the Victorian age with a characteristic mix of patterns.

Sometimes the simplest embellishment is the most effective. Here a trompe l'oeil plaster molding adds the perfect finish to upholstered walls; it is one of many trompe l'oeil borders available.

Here's a room that is sure to delight. A sweet wallpaper border divides painted earth from sky. This is an easy way to add lots of detail; it would be difficult to stencil a similar effect.

Windows and Doors

Y ou must approach windows and doors from several angles when you decorate. First, they are part of your home's architecture. Exterior doors and windows are seen from the street and also within, so their character is doubly important; they must suit the architectural style of the building as well as your personal preferences. They must work, too. They open and close; they allow entry and egress; they provide ventilation; and they incorporate exterior views into the interior.

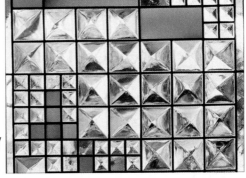

The location, number, and type of windows and doors control the amount and nature of natural light, and affect your home's security and temperature stability. Do some research when you are choosing doors and windows to be sure the styles you select will suit your home both practically and aesthetically.

A generous half-round room expands both view and living space. This one was constructed from stock windows, and features fixed and casement units that have been painted white. Divided lights give a period feel to the room. The semisheer Roman shades fall in a gentle scallop— a nice transition from the traditional bow window wall to the more contemporary cedar-lined ceiling.

STYLE OPTIONS FOR WINDOWS

WINDOWS ARE PART of a home's architectural identity, immediately conveying period and style. They also have a tremendous environmental influence, affecting the light, ventilation, and temperature of the interior—and the comfort of the occupants. Today efficient windows to suit almost any architectural style are readily available, so you can let the sun shine in with wit, elegance, grace, and practicality.

A large picture window provides a seamless view and makes a room seem larger. The closer the window is to the floor—and the less trim and drapery it supports—the more you feel you can walk right through it. Note the compact vertical blinds used here; when open they nearly disappear.

Above left: Interesting divided lights and plain broad trim give these ganged casement windows an Arts and Crafts feeling. A small custom unit, which has trim of the same scale, draws attention to the peaked ceiling. White Roman shades match the trim and stack at the window sill so as not to obscure the muntins. Soft blue-gray walls echo the color of sky and distant trees.

Above right: This pretty bedroom in a turn-of-the-century seaside home features new double-hung windows with removable grilles to make cleaning easier. A fixed pentagon window takes advantage of the raised ceiling. Bull's-eye corner blocks in the casing around all the windows give a traditional finish to the two-light sash.

OPTIONS FOR GLASS

Windows of clear glass are the norm for most of us, but there are many glazing options. Leaded glass adds a decorative pattern; when stained it adds color, and perhaps a picture. Colored or frosted glass enhances privacy. Traditional bevels add elegance. Decoratively glazed windows often look best without additional dressing.

Geometric multicolored glazing adds a decorative touch. Here, the pattern enhances the view instead of obscuring it. Walls and casing are painted in the same palette.

Stained glass offers privacy while allowing light to pass. It is usually reserved for exterior, sun-touched glazing. This interior door glows when the room beyond is lighted.

Custom glazing can be as unique or idiosyncratic as the surrounding architecture. In this very contemporary home, a curved insert of frosted glass provides privacy and keeps a long passageway from turning into a dark hole.

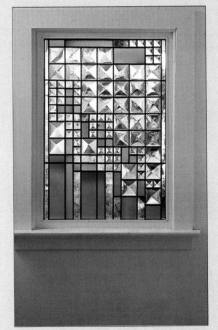

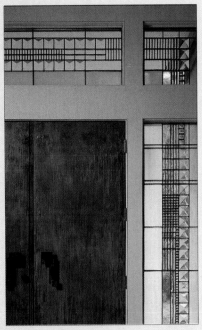

This pretty leaded glass window is ever changing and always intriguing. Bevels add texture and create a constant play of light. Stained panes contribute jewel-like color.

Divided-light windows with an allover pattern of leaded rounds bring an Old-World charm and diffuse the view. Colored glass plates are a pretty accessory.

Hundreds of small beveled panes create a marvelously textured and translucent surround for this entryway, echoing the verdigris finish of the copper-clad door.

When the morning sun shines through this kitchen window, the room dances with little blue diamonds. Leaded glazing like this adds character to the room and the view. The Dutch door is a nice touch.

Right: When wall space is limited, or privacy an issue, consider using clerestory windows. Placed above eye level, usually in a row, they allow light to enter, obstruct the view in from outside, and cast infinitely interesting shadow patterns to play on adjacent walls and floors. Here an elegant spiral stairway leads the eye up to a row of fixed windows that light both foyer and second-floor landing.

Opposite: Small single windows are like doorways to secret places. They frame just a glimpse and focus just a small beam onto floor or wall. Small windows work best when they relate to the adjacent architecture—in a bay, under stairs, above a counter—otherwise they may look isolated or out of proportion. This charming arched casement, in a corner under a low ceiling, is balanced by a painting.

Stock windows come in all shapes and sizes. When combined creatively they are decorative in their own right. Here gracefully divided arched windows give an elegant finish to a contemporary great room. One is flanked by rectangular units to fit in the breakfast nook gable while others are paired on an interior wall. The custom skylight echoes the muntin pattern.

WINDOW WORDS

APRON: An applied interior trim piece that runs beneath the unit, below the sill.

CASEMENT: A window with a frame that hinges on the side, like a door.

CASING: Wooden window trim, especially interior, added by owner or contractor. Head casing runs at top; side casings flank unit.

CLADDING: A protective sheath of aluminum or vinyl covering a window's exterior wood surfaces.

FLASHING: Thin sheets, usually metal, that make window or skylight edges watertight.

GLAZING: The window pane itself— glass, acrylic plastic, or other clear or translucent material. May be one, two (i.e., double-glazed), or even three layers thick.

GRILLE: A decorative, removable grate that makes an expanse of glass look like many smaller panes.

JAMB: The outside frame that surrounds sash or glazing. An extension jamb adds depth to a window to match a thick wall.

LIGHTS: Separately framed panes of glass in a multipane window. Each light is held by muntins.

LOW EMISSIVITY, LOW-E: Has been treated to improve the thermal performance of glass, especially in double-glazed windows, at little extra cost.

MULLION: A vertical dividing piece that separates multiple windows.

MUNTIN: Slender strip of wood framing a pane of glass in a multipane (divided light) window.

R-VALUE: Measure of a material's ability to insulate (retard heat flow); the higher the number, the lower heating or cooling bills can be.

SASH: A window frame surrounding glass. May be fixed or operable.

SILL: Interior or exterior shelf below window sash. Interior sill may be called a *stool*.

TRANSOM: A window over a door, or sometimes another window. May be fixed or operable.

U-VALUE: Measure of the energy efficiency of all the materials in the window; the lower the u-value, the better.

WINDOW SEATS

Who doesn't relish the idea of withdrawing to a cozy window seat to contemplate the rain? Window seats can be intimately draped, set into a niche or bay, or long enough to seat a crowd. They can be formal, funky, feminine— or whatever suits.

A corner window, offering security and an expansive view, is an ideal spot for a window seat. This one, painted white to fit unobtrusively into the decor, has handy drawers and is topped with lots of plump pillows.

A niche with grand casement windows and formal draperies offers a private spot for contemplation or tea. The handwoven shade diffuses the light.

With a high window you can build a high-backed upholstered seat, which seems extra cozy and inviting. Here, jewel-tone upholstery complements the beveled glass.

A quirky triangular niche holds an ample seat where you can sit cross-legged or curl up with a loved one. Rich, off-beat colors and whimsical pillows set a festive mood.

This graceful manufactured bow window was designed with the window seat in mind. The end windows are shorter so there is wall support for the throw pillows. The open bays under the seats show off treasures.

A row of windows in a great room positively cries out for a comfortable banquette, which offers maximum seating for minimum floor space. A long bench in an open room can carry bold mixed and matched fabrics.

STYLE OPTIONS FOR DOORS

"WELCOME" AND "KEEP OUT" are the dual messages of a door, which should look like part of your decor, and work to ensure privacy. Like windows, doors are part of the home's architecture. This is more true—and more problematic—with exterior doors, which set the tone from both public and private view, than for interior ones. However, there are many styles to choose from: sliding, swinging; single, double—take your pick.

Below: You must pass through an enclosed porch to reach the courtyard beyond this formal entry. Matching sets of French doors, topped with half-round windows, set an elegant, symmetrical stage; they allow light to penetrate the inside room while the porch roof blocks the glare.

Above: Sleek, sturdy French doors, built from steel, bring light and access to a contemporary kitchen. The brass cremone bolts are not only beautiful—they help secure the narrow door stiles. Doors such as these, which have no additional trim, seem light and airy but may be difficult to weatherproof.

Arched doorways soften a space and carry the eye upward. These pretty panel doors connect a kitchen to a dining area; the slatted sections provide a glimpse through and let conversation float from one area to the other. Narrow double doors such as these require less floor space to swing open. You might want to hang them with hinges that swing in either direction.

Pocket doors offer a clean, uncluttered solution to door-swing headaches—the door slides into the wall. This rectangular door looks arched, but it is not. The doorway is arched, and the curved top door rail accentuates the illusion. The wall in which a pocket door slides must be framed to accommodate it; these doors cannot be added to conventional walls.

Opposite above: Louvered doors create a feeling of privacy while allowing filtered light, air, and sound to pass through. They convey an aura of coolness in a warm or sultry climate. They are often used on closets, but there is no reason not to use them on room entries as long as soundproofing is not a concern. Here they make a pleasant transition between public and private areas.

Opposite below: Shoji panels are an appropriate door choice for a Japanese-style house. This bathroom features traditional sliding panels as well as fixed units set into conventional swinging doors. The beautiful vertical-grain fir frames have a clear finish, and the striking black trim shows off the panels to advantage.

STYLE OPTIONS FOR SKYLIGHTS

A SKYLIGHT CAN transform a cramped space into a spacious one, a dull room into a dramatic one. Skylights can be fixed, or operable for ventilation. They can let in lots of heat as well as light, so be prepared to fit them with shades (these can be electronically controlled for hard-to-reach heights). Skylights can be problematic to weatherproof; purchase the best quality you can afford and have them properly installed.

The sloping roof of this dramatic living area is glazed with a large expanse of diffusing acrylic. The individual "skylights" are formed by a floating ceiling grid, which also houses overhead lights. You could create a similar effect by installing conventional skylights at regular intervals.

In a room with no windows, a skylight brings welcome daylight. The skylight in this vanity corridor casts light on a plant niche above the makeup table. The mirrored walls make the most of the light coming through the skylight, and make the space seem larger than it is.

Skylights also provide a great view of the sky—especially nice on a starry night. These roof-peak panels shed light on the room below, while handsome trusses lead the eye up and out. Panels such as these must be custom-fabricated.

If you are installing windows or skylights as part of your redecorating, refer to the drawings to help you position them, and consider the points listed below as you choose them.

- Light
- Ventilation
- View
- Privacy
- Energy conservation
- Angle of skylight shaft

EFFECT OF EXPOSURE

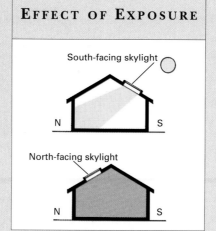

A south-facing skylight admits maximum light and heat year round. This is different from south-facing windows, which admit maximum light and heat in winter but not in summer. A north-facing skylight admits even, indirect light.

LIGHT SHAFTS

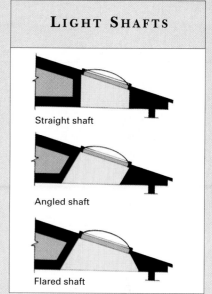

If there is an attic or crawl space above the skylight, you will need a shaft through it to let the light in; the shaft can be straight or angled.

WINDOW HEIGHT GUIDELINES

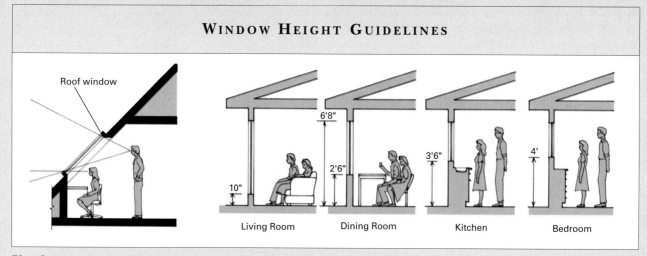

Plan for easy viewing from a standing or seated position, whether through a roof window or vertical window. Adjust heights for built-ins or to ensure privacy.

STYLE OPTIONS FOR GLASS WALLS

WINDOW WALLS dramatically link a landscape to an interior. Whether they feature large panes of glass or small, their structural support imposes a pattern on the view, the façade, and the room; this pattern becomes part of the decor. When you plan a window wall you should consider issues of privacy and unwanted light, since an interesting window wall may not work well (from inside or out) with a window treatment.

An impressive window wall and skylights create a wonderful conservatory effect. Many manufacturers offer connecting hardware that allows you to design a wall using complementary operable and fixed window units.

A two-story window wall, flanked by glazed doors, forms the multipaned centerpiece of this entrance hall. It allows sun to flood both the main floor and an upstairs landing, and makes landscape views possible from either. The glass-topped table is a nice touch. It offers a spot for display without obstructing the view.

Informal wood and glass doors lead from this glass-walled foyer to a lovely landscape; seamless corner glazing allows an unobstructed 180-degree view. The floor and ceiling flow smoothly from indoors to out, lit by the small skylight that spans the foyer and overhang.

Window walls don't need to soar to be effective. The ceiling in this room is a standard height and the floor-to-near-ceiling glazing on adjacent walls merges the woodland setting with the interior. This wall combines fixed upper panes with lower awning windows that open for ventilation.

Wall Coverings

Walls serve as the backdrop for all the other furnishings in a room; they can be key players or supporting characters. You can cover them with color bright or muted, with patterns bold or subtle, with texture soft or rough. You can camouflage or accentuate your architecture, transform the character of the space, or create a neutral cocoon. You can treat all the walls in your home in the same manner, or each room— or each wall within a room—differently. A change in wall coverings

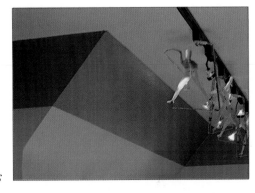

is a simple, effective way to update your environment.

Some wall coverings are easy and inexpensive to change; others require skill and a sizeable investment. Look at samples in the room in a variety of lights, next to your furnishings or other swatches. And do your math before making purchases—there is nothing worse than running short of something that was custom-ordered.

It takes an innovative eye to choose a conventional two-color scheme and use it to contrast rather than conform with architecture. Here bold, even stripes run around a room in complete disregard to structural planes and angles. The unusual effect is interesting and surprisingly successful.

PAINT FOR EFFECT

STRAIGHTFORWARD APPLICATION OF PAINT to a wall colors the background of a decor in an easy—and easily changed—manner. But an expanse of solid color may not be what you are looking for. Faux-finish effects with subtle color variations add depth and life, and many of them are easy and fun to do (little imperfections are part of their charm). Borders add character, murals and trompe l'oeil scenes transform.

Opposite: Representational, or trompe l'oeil, wallpainting can conjure up an environment that isn't really there. It requires a deft hand and is usually done by a professional. Two potted wisteria vines, perpetually a-bloom, decorate this bay in place of draperies, which would look heavy and block light and air. The coordinated shades can be lowered to cut direct glare.

Below: To enter this young lady's room is to enter a fairy-tale world. The walls were painted with delicate flora and charming costumed animals in a style reminiscent of children's book illustrations. This mural is evocative rather than narrative, but traditional wallpaintings that literally tell a story can be every bit as wonderful.

The dining room in this city apartment was painted to resemble the aged stucco you might find in a centuries-old Mediterranean home. A faux finish such as this is achieved with subtle paint glazes that are manipulated with a rag, plastic wrap, or crumpled brown paper—and more patience than skill.

The faux finish in this eclectic bathroom was inspired by visits to medieval palaces. Layers of earthy colors were applied to the walls, followed by fleur-de-lis stenciled in pewter metallic paint, and a glaze applied with stiff plastic. A hand-painted star map covers the vaulted ceiling.

Opposite: A celestial theme comes to life in this colorful nursery. The designers splashed purple glazing across the ceiling and trim, streaked on some faux wainscoting, and finished with a field of yellow rag-painted walls. Pink accents and whimsical gold stars complete the effect.

ABOUT PAINT

WASHES & GLAZES

Most decorative painting techniques are done with washes or glazes. A wash is watered-down latex paint, and a glaze is thinned, translucent oil-base or acrylic color. The quick-drying washes are suitable for the simpler techniques, such as sponging. The more complex techniques requiring a buildup of color, such as marbling, are best accomplished with glazes, which stay wet longer than washes and give you more time to manipulate them before they dry.

Oil or water-base?

Oil glazes, the traditional medium of decorative painters, stay wet and workable longer than either washes or acrylic glazes, and produce a wonderfully translucent finish. Mistakes are easy to correct—just dab on paint thinner and wipe off the paint. Note, however, that handling oil-base paints and thinners requires care because of the chemicals and fumes involved.

Acrylic glazes and latex washes are easy to use—they're mixed and cleaned up with water. Although water-base finishes generally don't last as long as oil-base ones, you can always apply a clear coating to protect the finish.

Making washes & glazes

It's not difficult to mix your own wash or glaze. Simply follow the instructions and recipes given on this page.

• Washes are extremely simple to make—you just mix a pint of ordinary latex from a paint store with water.

• To make a glaze, it's easiest to start with a transparent commercial glaze—basically paint without any pigment. Then add paint from a paint store—alkyd for an oil glaze, acrylic for an acrylic glaze. The intensity of the color will be thinned by the commercial glaze, producing a translucent paint.

• You can also use paint from an art supply store or crafts shop, but you'll need some expertise in choosing colors. Japan colors or artist's oils are compatible with oil glazes, artist's acrylics with acrylic glazes or latex washes. Use universal tints to color any medium.

• To the colored glaze, add the appropriate solvent—paint thinner for an oil glaze and water for an acrylic glaze. The solvent dilutes the paint so that it can be applied in very thin coats. To extend the drying time slightly, you can add a retarding agent to an acrylic glaze.

The following recipes are just a starting point. Decorative painting isn't an exact science. In fact, it's more akin to cooking than to chemistry. Don't be afraid to experiment as you become more practiced and confident.

Latex Wash

You can vary the recipe so that water makes up from 10 to 90 percent of the mixture. The more paint you use, the more durable the finish.

> 1 part latex paint
> 2 parts water

Oil Glaze

A good general recipe for beginners, this glaze stays wet even if you work slowly. For faster drying and a harder finish, use less commercial oil glaze and more paint thinner.

> 1 part commercial oil glaze
> 1 part alkyd paint
> 1 part paint thinner

Acrylic Glaze #1

This glaze recipe is suitable for ragging, sponging, and simple marbling. Change the proportions to 5 parts commercial acrylic glaze, 1 part paint, and 1 part water for decorative techniques requiring greater translucency, such as dragging, wood graining, and more sophisticated marbling.

> 1 part commercial acrylic glaze
> 2 parts acrylic paint
> 1 part water
> 2-4 oz. retarder per gallon
>   (optional)

Acrylic Glaze #2

Use this recipe if you don't have easy access to a commercial acrylic glaze. Look for acrylic gel medium in an art supply store.

> 1 part acrylic gel medium
> 1 part acrylic paint
> 2 parts water
> 2-4 oz. retarder per gallon
>   (optional)

Interior Paints for all Surfaces

SURFACE	PRIME OR FIRST COAT	FINISH COAT(S)	COMMENTS
NEW WALLBOARD	Seal surface with PVA (polyvinyl acetate) sealer; let dry thoroughly.	Apply two coats of latex or alkyd flat or enamel paint. Sand lightly between enamel coats.	Don't use an alkyd primer—it will raise nap in paper.
NEW PLASTER	Seal surface with a vinyl acrylic wall primer; let dry thoroughly.	Apply two coats of latex or alkyd flat or enamel paint. Sand lightly between enamel coats.	You can use PVA sealer instead of vinyl acrylic wall primer, but you'll need more to do the same job.
EXISTING WALLBOARD OR PLASTER	Treat small stains with a white-pigmented shellac, larger ones with a quick-drying alkyd primer. Spot-prime patches with PVA sealer or finish paint diluted 10 percent. If surface is more than 5 years old or there is a big color change, prime entire surface, using a vinyl acrylic wall primer over a latex finish, an alkyd primer over an oil-base finish.	Apply two coats of latex or alkyd flat or enamel paint. Sand lightly between enamel coats.	When applying an enamel finish over an existing flat finish, ensure uniform sheen by priming entire surface.
BARE WOOD TO BE PAINTED	Use an alkyd enamel undercoater. (On fir, you can use a latex enamel undercoater since it doesn't bleed.) Let dry overnight.	Apply a first coat of latex or alkyd enamel paint thinned 10 percent with appropriate solvent (water for latex and paint thinner for alkyd); let dry thoroughly. Sand lightly; then apply a second, undiluted coat.	An enamel finish is usually recommended for wood.
PAINTED WOOD TO BE REPAINTED	Chip away loose, flaking paint and sand smooth. Spot-prime bare wood spots with a white-pigmented shellac; let dry for 30 minutes.	Apply a first coat of undiluted latex or alkyd enamel paint; let dry thoroughly. Sand lightly; then apply a second coat and let dry overnight.	An enamel finish is usually recommended for wood.
BARE WOOD TO BE STAINED	Fill holes with natural latex wood patch before staining. For uniform stain absorption on soft woods, use a stain-controlling sealer. Stain desired color; let dry overnight. If surface feels rough, apply a quick-drying sanding sealer and sand lightly.	Apply a first coat of varnish thinned 10 percent with paint thinner; let dry thoroughly. Sand lightly; then apply a second, undiluted coat and let dry for 24 hours.	Polyurethane or other clear finishes can be applied over a stain and some sanding sealers; refer to manufacturer's directions.
BARE WOOD TO BE COATED WITH A CLEAR FINISH	Apply varnish, polyurethane, or other clear finish in desired sheen.	Apply one or two additional coats of clear finish, sanding lightly between coats.	Test coating on an inconspicuous spot. Thin first coat, if necessary, for easier application (see label).
MASONRY	Use acrylic or latex block filler. For a waterproof surface, follow with a hydrostatic coating; if it's going over a previous coating, consult a dealer—all coatings aren't compatible.	Apply two coats of latex or alkyd flat or enamel paint. Sand lightly between enamel coats.	First remove any powdery crust. Wash with muriatic acid, rinse thoroughly, and let dry for 72 hours.
METAL	Remove dirt with vinegar; rinse. Sand off rust; prime. Use rust-inhibitive primer on new metal that will rust, latex metal primer on galvanized metal, conventional metal primer on aluminum.	Apply two coats of latex or alkyd enamel in desired sheen or colored polyurethane. Don't sand between coats.	Flat wall paint isn't recommended.

PAINTED MOLDINGS

You can turn to architectural detail to add fine points to a room's character, and moldings are a great place to find quirks, humor, or dignity. Some rooms are blessed with wonderful molded embellishments that can be highlighted with color. If yours is not, don't despair—paint some on.

Fancy finishing brings a vintage bathroom up to date. A beige glaze was applied over a black background and dabbed with crumpled paper.

A wonderful three-dimensional plaster molding tops the rough walls of this wine-country home. The details are picked out with soft washes of paint. If you are not inclined to do this yourself, begin with ready-glazed molding tiles.

Nothing could be more contemporary than large picture windows framed in meticulously painted faux columns. Whether you consider them to be updates or antiquities is a matter of semantics—there is no denying they're fun.

Here the molding *is* three-dimensional, but marble it is not. Cleverly veined with a feather dipped in paint, the trim adds an elaborate finish to this room. Marble comes in many colorations; imitate your favorite.

Moldings don't have to be fancy or faux to have an impact. Sometimes a straightforward clean contrast is strikingly effective, as it is here, where sharp white archways enliven a staid, deep taupe wall.

WALLPAPER FOR EFFECT

IT IS HARD TO SURPASS the versatility of wallpaper. Depending on its color and pattern, wallpaper can take center stage or simply stand as a subtle background for the other furnishings. It is available in myriad colors, styles, textures, and patterns (often with coordinated borders) in a variety of materials, from durable vinyl to delicate hand-screened paper. With so many options, you can use wallpaper in virtually any room.

Neatly striped wallpaper is a classic and foolproof choice for adding a little noncompetitive character to a room. When one of the colors is white, striped paper looks especially crisp. In this room the white freshens an otherwise muted palette; the pink is picked up from the fabric.

Opposite above: Lattice-patterned wallpaper is the perfect background for a collection of majolica plates; it complements the room's European country flavor without calling attention to itself. Trellis-like lattice patterns are a good choice when walls are a bit irregular, as slight distortions will not be too obvious.

Opposite below: Proportion and balance are the key to working with bold allover patterns. Large florals and geometrics, if not used carefully, can be overwhelming. This lush floral works well because smaller scale patterns pick up its colors, and restrained furniture, plain floors, and white woodwork provide a restful counterpoint.

Although this surface resembles the painting technique known as dragging, it is actually wallpaper. The subtle striping provides a supportive but not distracting background for artwork and is particularly appropriate in an Early American decor. One great advantage of wallpaper is that you can achieve all sorts of painterly effects with no mess and no talent.

Torn paper applied in overlapping layers on a bathroom wall simulates the look of marble without the expense. You can create your own customized wallpaper from other found materials, such as art prints, doilies, blueprints, childrens' drawings, photographs, even plain brown paper.

The trompe l'oeil design of this library wallpaper makes a tiny space seem larger—and more interesting. Note how the "wood" border at the base of the books reinforces the design's realism. The paper's rich, traditional colors and feeling are echoed in the medieval tapestry-style throw pillows.

ABOUT WALLPAPER

CHOOSING WALLPAPER

Often, the use the room receives will suggest the best material for the wall covering. For example, although most children's areas need only washable paper, a scrubbable one will stand up better to rough treatment and thorough cleaning. The material content of a wall covering is a determining factor not only in its durability and cleanability, but also in its appearance, cost, installation, and ease of removal.

The back of a wallpaper sample usually contains information on the wallpaper's content, whether it's washable or scrubbable, and whether it can be stripped or peeled from the wall. You can also check there to learn the size of its pattern repeat. Before purchasing a large quantity, get a sample or buy one roll and look at it in your room with your other furnishings or samples.

Vinyls

The most popular wallpapers, especially for do-it-yourselfers, have some vinyl content. Vinyl's durability and strength make these papers relatively easy to install; they're also easy to maintain.

FABRIC-BACKED VINYL: Has a vinyl top layer and an undersurface of fiberglass or cheesecloth. The sturdiest kind of wallpaper, fabric-backed vinyl is washable, often scrubbable, and usually strippable. Compared with other papers, it's also more moisture-resistant and less likely to tear if a wall cracks. Fabric-backed vinyl usually comes unpasted because it's often too heavy to roll well if prepasted.

PAPER-BACKED VINYL: Has a vinyl top layer with a paper rather than fabric backing. This makes the wall covering lighter, so paper-backed vinyl comes prepasted. It's often peelable and washable.

EXPANDED VINYL: Has a three-dimensional effect; is paper-backed. It's often designed to look like another surface, such as rough plaster, granite, textured paint, or grass cloth. It's especially suitable for walls that aren't perfectly smooth.

VINYL-COATED PAPER: Looks like paper and not vinyl, so lends an air of sophistication to light-use areas. Even vinyl-coated papers that are labeled washable can stain and tear easily .

Textiles

Textile wall coverings come in many colors and textures, from very casual to elegantly formal. They're usually made of cotton, linen, or other natural plant fibers, or polyester, often bonded to a paper-type backing. Some textiles require liner paper underneath; many should be installed only by a skilled paperhanger. Keep in mind that most textiles fray easily and are not washable, though most will accept a spray-on stain repellent. Some are peelable.

GRASS CLOTH: A traditional favorite among textile wall coverings; available with threads arranged vertically, horizontally, or in a woven pattern.

HEMP: Similar to grass cloth but has thinner fibers.

BURLAP: Rugged appearance, woven.

MOIRÉ OR PRINTED PATTERNS: Sophisticated patterns on dyed fabrics.

Solid paper

Whether they're inexpensive or costly, wall coverings made of solid paper without any vinyl tear easily.

HAND-SCREENED: Each color in a hand-screened paper is applied with a separate handmade and hand-placed silk screen. This process makes hand-screened papers more expensive than the majority of other wallpapers, which are machine printed. Hand-screened papers are difficult to handle and are usually hung by professionals.

FOILS: Have a reflective surface, can brighten up a small, dark space. Wrinkle easily, require an absolutely smooth wall surface and special installation. Usually hung by professionals.

FLOCKED PAPERS: Have textured patterns, resemble damask or cut velvet. Difficult to work with, usually hung by professionals.

MURALS: Depict nature or some historic event. Open up a room, particularly if the strips are hung across a large expanse of wall. Or, for a little less drama, try hanging a single-panel mural in the middle of a large wall; on either side hang a paper that matches the mural's background. May require professional installation.

DETERMINING QUANTITIES

Be generous when you estimate wallpaper quantities—rolls printed at different times may not provide an exact color match, so be sure to order enough the first time.

To determine how much wallpaper to buy, measure the walls to be covered; use a long steel tape measure and mark down the dimensions: Measure the height and width of each wall (including openings). For a quick and generally reliable estimate of the number of rolls you'll need, use the chart below (the figures assume an 8-foot ceiling). For European rolls, multiply the number of rolls by 1.25. Deduct one roll for every two openings.

Quantity Guide

DISTANCE AROUND ROOM (IN FEET)	NUMBER OF ROLLS FOR WALL	NUMBER OF YARDS FOR BORDER	NUMBER OF ROLLS FOR CEILING
30	8	11	2
32	8	12	2
34	10	13	4
36	10	13	4
38	10	14	4
40	10	15	4
42	12	15	4
44	12	16	4
46	12	17	6
48	14	17	6
50	14	18	6
52	14	19	6
54	14	19	6
56	14	20	8
58	16	21	8
60	16	21	8

Exact measurement method

- Multiply the height and width of each wall; add the figures together. Deduct 15 square feet for every average-sized door or window. For larger or unusually shaped openings, deduct the exact square footage.
- An American single roll contains 36 square feet of material; a European single roll contains 29 square feet. To allow for cutting and trimming, figure on 30 usable square feet per American roll, 25 per European roll.
- Divide the total square footage of wall space by the square footage of one roll to determine the total number required. Round up to a complete roll.

Allowing for pattern repeats

To estimate accurately, you'll also have to consider the wallpaper pattern. With a random pattern, one that doesn't repeat vertically in any regular fashion, use the estimating methods described above.

- For paper with a straight or drop match, note the repeat height on the back of the sample. Divide the wall height (in inches) by the pattern repeat (in inches); round up any fractional remainder to the next highest number. For example, a 96-inch wall height divided by an 18-inch pattern repeat gives you 5.33 repeats, rounded up to 6.
- Multiply this number by the length of each repeat to get your "working height." (In our example, 6 repeats multiplied by an 18-inch repeat gives you a working height of 108 inches.)
- To calculate the number of rolls you need, figure square footage based on the working height, rather than actual room height.

Estimating for multiple papers

If you're hanging more than one paper, for instance one above a chair rail and another below, make an estimate for each paper.

- Figure how many rolls you'd need if you were using only one paper. Then measure the vertical distance each paper will cover on the wall. Divide this by the total height to get that paper's percentage of the total wall height. To find the number of rolls needed of each paper, multiply the total number of rolls you'd need by each percentage.

Estimating for borders

- Measure the width (in feet) of all areas you're covering. Divide by 3 to get the number of yards needed. Borders usually come in rolls 5 yards long. If you're planning to miter corners around doors and windows, add some extra.

Inspecting your wallpaper

Check that the pattern numbers are correct on all the rolls. Every roll should also have the same run number or dye-lot number.

- Carefully unroll each roll and inspect its entire length. Flaws to look for include uneven ink, wrinkled edges, and poor color registrations. Lay the rolls next to each other on a table—the pattern on the left edge of one roll should match the pattern on the right edge of another.
- If you find any problems talk with your dealer right away. If the problem is small and the pattern is in limited supply, you may be able to work around the flaw.
- Store wallpaper in a dry area until you're ready to hang it. Lay rolls horizontally, and do not place anything heavy on top of them.

WALLPAPER TERMS

BOLT: Two or more continuous rolls of wallpaper in a single package.

BOOKING: Relaxing a pasted strip by folding pasted side against itself so the ends overlap and the edges align.

BORDER: A decorative strip, most commonly used to trim a wall at the ceiling line, at chair-rail height, or around doors and windows.

BUTT SEAM: A method of seaming two wallpaper strips by pushing their edges together firmly.

DOUBLE-CUT SEAM: A method of seaming two wallpaper strips by overlapping their edges and cutting through both strips.

DROP MATCH: A pattern in which the design element at one edge of a strip is half a repeat lower than at the other edge. The design elements at the top are alike on every other strip.

LAP SEAM: A method of seaming two strips of wallpaper by lapping one edge over another.

LINER PAPER: Blank paper stock hung under wallpaper in order to smooth wall surfaces, absorb excess moisture, and provide a breathable layer between a nonporous wall covering and the wall.

NONPOROUS WALL COVERING: A wall covering that water or water-soluble adhesive cannot penetrate. Foils and papers with vinyl content are examples of nonporous wall coverings.

PATTERN REPEAT: The vertical distance between one design element on a pattern and the next occurrence of that design element.

PEELABLE WALLPAPER: Wallpaper that can be removed from the wall by peeling off the top layer. This leaves a thin residue of paper and adhesive, which is removable with water.

POROUS WALL COVERING: A wall covering that water or water-soluble adhesive can penetrate. Most textiles and papers without vinyl are examples.

PREPASTED WALLPAPER: Wallpaper that has been factory coated with water-soluble adhesive. You activate the paste by soaking the paper in water for the recommended time.

PRETRIMMED WALLPAPER: Wallpaper from which the selvage edge has been trimmed at the factory.

RANDOM MATCH: A pattern or texture having no design elements that need to be matched between adjoining strips.

RUN, OR DYE-LOT, NUMBER: The number given to each separate printing of a pattern. Each printing can vary in color and intensity.

SCRUBBABLE WALL COVERING: A wall covering durable enough to be scrubbed with a soft brush and mild soap.

SELVAGE: The unpatterned side edge of wallpaper that protects it during shipping and handling. The selvage must be trimmed before the wallpaper is hung.

SIZE, ALSO SIZING: A liquid coating applied to wall surfaces to seal the surface, help the adhesive grip the wall, and allow the installer to move the wallpaper into position more easily.

STRAIGHT MATCH: A pattern in which the design flows directly across the strips, so the design elements at the top of adjoining matched strips are the same on both strips.

STRIP: A length of wallpaper cut to fit the area it will cover.

STRIPPABLE WALLPAPER: Wallpaper that can be removed from the wall by hand without tearing or leaving any paper residue. (It may leave some adhesive.)

WASHABLE WALLPAPER: Wallpaper that can be cleaned with a solution of mild soap and water.

FABRIC FOR EFFECT

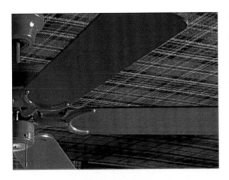

SOMETHING SPECIAL HAPPENS when you cover your walls with fabric. Because it has texture, fabric lends softness and warmth to a room in a way no other wall covering does. It can be applied flush, stapled over batting for more dimension, or even shirred or draped. Fabric also offers a good way to mask problem wall surfaces. Depending upon the material and application, fabric-covered walls can look formal or informal.

Above: The synthetic suede that covers these walls reinforces the softness of the plump oversize sofa. Light spilling onto the walls is gently diffused by the velvety texture. This is a soothing contemporary room, with nothing hard or slick about it.

The elegant black fixtures in this bath are nicely set off by a restrained, slightly textured striped fabric. Dark colors tend to drink up light, which can be a problem in a bathroom, but sconces, overhead downlights, and strip lights assure adequate light.

By working with a coordinated line of fabric you can base your decorating plan on diverse elements that are guaranteed to work together. Traditional French country prints feature allover designs with wonderful companion borders. Here upholstered walls enclose—and enhance—a pretty four-poster hung with matching draperies; the border at the ceiling pulls the look together with a complementary finish.

Moiré panels offer a restrained and lovely counterpoint to rich moldings in a formal setting. They make this room lighter than a floor-to-ceiling expanse of mahogany paneling would. A matching double welt trims the panels, hiding raw edges and staples with understated elegance. With the right components a contrasting welt would be an effective, but more important, trim.

Opposite: A bold red plaid may be an unexpected choice for turn-of-the-century kitchen walls, but it certainly sets the mood of this eclectic decor. There is a lot going on in this room, but large furnishings and wonderful rich colors balance the exuberant tartan walls and ceiling very effectively—you can't think for a moment that this chef will make bland meals.

FABRIC COVERED WALLS

CHOOSING A TECHNIQUE

Three techniques for applying fabric to walls—upholstering, stapling, and pasting—are described here. To decide which technique is best for you, think about the look you want to achieve and the amount of time and effort you're willing to spend on the project. All three techniques require approximately the same amount of fabric.

Pasting

Pasting fabric on walls differs from most other wall-covering techniques in that you apply adhesive to the wall, not to the wall covering. Fabric pasted on walls is resistant to steam and can be easily removed without causing damage to the wall; any paste residue left on the walls can be washed off.

- Before you decide to paste fabric on your walls, consider the following drawbacks: This application reveals any bumps, cracks, or other wall damage, so walls must be perfectly smooth. Also, colored walls must be given a coat of white primer so light-colored fabrics won't appear tinted.

Stapling

For this simple application, you stitch together panels of fabric and then staple them to the walls. Trim, usually double welt, is used to finish the edges.

- If you want to simulate the appearance of upholstered walls and increase the insulating and acoustic qualities of the wall, choose a quilted fabric.
- Test the wall to see if it is suitable for stapling. Generally the small holes left by the staples can be filled with paint or spackle if you decide to remove the fabric later. If the staples can't puncture the surface, or if they leave large holes and chip the wall, you can mount furring strips to provide a good working surface.

Upholstering

Covering walls with fabric over batting takes more time than stapling or pasting it directly on the surface, but upholstered walls are worth the work. Batting cushions the fabric, provides soundproofing and insulation, and gives the fabric a soft, luxurious appearance. Trim, usually double welt, is used to finish the edges.

- Upholstered walls usually conceal wall imperfections, such as cracks and uneven surfaces.
- Upholstered walls are not recommended for kitchens and bathrooms, where grease and steam are problems.
- You can upholster ceilings, too, but it's best to do so in a small room, as you will have to stretch the fabric tightly and anchor it in several places to prevent sagging.

CHOOSING FABRIC

Deciding on a fabric may seem as challenging as the work of putting it up on the wall. Before you commit to one, consider both its appearance and its suitability for the application you have in mind. Get a swatch or buy a small amount and look at it in your room with your other furnishings or samples. Fabrics should be firmly woven and opaque. If they are bulky, it will be difficult to make self-welting.

- Home decorating fabrics are excellent choices. Available in widths up to 60 inches, these fabrics are usually treated with a repellent that inhibits stains and dust collection. Also, they're printed with pattern overlaps at the selvages, making it easy to match the pattern at the seams.
- If you're upholstering or stapling, you can also consider flat bed sheets. (Their size makes them hard to handle if you're pasting.) Less expensive than home decorating fabrics, sheets come in numerous colors and designs.
- Be cautious when selecting a printed fabric. If the print is off-grain—veering at an angle from the lengthwise threads—it will appear misaligned when hung.
- Fabrics with allover designs are the easiest to work with, because the pattern can help camouflage wall imperfections and uneven ceiling lines. They also show less soil than those with large, open-ground patterns.
- Avoid stripes, plaids, and large geometric patterns for your first project, since any mistakes in application will be obvious.

DETERMINING YARDAGE

Before you make your purchases, take time to check and recheck the total yardage figures required for each material. These figures include a margin of safety that will ensure you'll have enough material to complete the project. It's always possible that the same pattern or dye lot won't be available later if you need more material.

Use a long steel tape measure to make your measurements. Mark the dimensions on paper—you'll need to use the figures to make the yardage calculations and to determine cutting lines. As you measure, keep in mind that each wall is to be covered with a separate fabric cover.

Width measurement

- Separately measure the width (in inches) of each wall you're planning to cover, unless you'll be working around an outside corner; in that case you'll use one fabric cover, starting it at one wall edge, wrapping it around the corner, and continuing to the far edge of the wall.
- To find the number of fabric panels required for one wall, divide the width of the wall by the usable width of the fabric, taking into account the amount of fabric taken up in seams (plan ½-inch seam allowances). If you are using sheets, use the width of the sheet. If your calculations result in a fraction, add a whole panel. This extra fabric width will give you some leeway to match the pattern at corners.

Height measurement

- Measure the height (in inches) of the same wall from the ceiling line (or lower edge of the ceiling molding) to the top of the base-board. Take this measurement in several places to check for variations; use the largest figure. Before choosing sheets, be sure your wall is no higher than the length of the sheet.
- Add 6 inches to the height measurement as insurance against errors. If the fabric has a pattern repeat, add the repeat length to the height measurement to allow for matching the pattern at the seams. Your final figure is the working height of the wall.

Total fabric yardage

- Multiply the working height figure by the number of fabric panels needed for the wall; divide this figure by 36 to convert to the number of yards of fabric required for the wall you've measured.
- Repeat the calculations for each wall you're covering. Add together the yardage for all the walls to determine total required. Add extra yardage if you plan to finish the walls with double welt (instructions for measuring for trim follow).

DETERMINING BATTING YARDAGE

To pad the walls, use ¾-inch bonded polyester batting. Available 48, 54, or 96 inches wide, batting can be purchased by the yard in large fabric stores or those specializing in home decorating fabrics, or by mail from sewing notions catalogs.

- To compute the amount of batting you'll need, measure (in inches) the exact height and width of the area to be covered; do not add extra inches.
- Total the width measurements of the walls and divide by the width of the batting to determine how many strips of batting you need; round up to the next whole number. Multiply this figure by the height of the wall, and divide by 36 to convert to the number of yards of batting required.
- Dimensions of large openings, such as sliding doors and picture windows, can be subtracted from your yardage figure, since batting can be pieced around openings.

MEASURING FOR TRIM

A double welt made of the same fabric as that on the wall or of a complementary fabric is the traditional finish. Or you can use heavy grosgrain ribbon (glue will show through lightweight ribbon), braid, or gimp in the same or contrasting color. Molding that's stained, painted, or wrapped with fabric also makes an attractive trim.

- Plan to use a continuous strip of trim (unless you're using molding) for the perimeter of the area to be covered. To determine how much trim you'll need, track in your mind a course that starts at an inconspicuous lower corner, travels completely around the upholstered area at floor level, goes up the wall at the starting corner, and travels around the top edge.
- Measure this distance and round up to the next half-yard to provide a margin of safety. Also measure around the edges of all unconnected openings, such as windows, that must be trimmed. Add all measurements together to determine the total yardage of finished welting or trim. If you do not know how to calculate the amount of fabric needed to make the determined amount of welting, ask your fabric vendor to assist you.

ECLECTIC WALL COVERINGS

When considering wall coverings, one's first thoughts are likely to be paint, paper, fabric, or paneling, but there are many other options that may be desirable for cosmetic, maintenance, or structural reasons. Whether you are building or remodeling, plan as far ahead as possible—some of these can't be added after the fact.

Poured concrete is structural, but in the right home it can be an effective background when left exposed. Here it smooths the transition from outdoors to indoors.

A magnificent basketweave of diagonally set glazed ceramic tile creates an imposing facade for this cooking station. The large tiles are a good proportion for this room.

Mirror is a terrific wall covering. It makes a space seem larger; additionally, when it reflects carefully composed surroundings, it establishes an intriguing environment—as here, where you *must* look twice.

Above: Marble tile makes a cool and elegant wall covering. Here contrasting varieties set in diamond and strip patterns accent the shape of the room.

Above right: Brick walls are often structural; they evoke converted factories, rowhouses with the plaster removed, or transitional spaces such as this passageway. Brick provides an instant basis for a color scheme.

Right: Nothing matches stainless steel as a sleek, elegant, and clean surface. Here a bold diamond pattern quilts a backsplash, breaking up the clinical expanse.

PANELING FOR EFFECT

THERE IS A STYLE OF PANELING to suit almost any decor. You can choose rustic boards, frame-and-panel designs with or without molding, or elaborate raised panels. You can cover an entire wall or choose waist- or shoulder-high wainscoting—or dress up a room with the simple addition of a chair or picture rail, or add a crown molding. Paneling can be made of fine or inexpensive wood; it can be painted or clear finished.

Above: High beamed ceilings, a beautiful fireplace, and a surrounding expanse of framed paneling topped by a dimensional picture molding give this room a grand presence. The woodwork was bleached and pickled.

Left: Beaded wainscoting was once common in bathrooms because it was more water-resistant than plaster walls. Today it adds a nostalgic charm to a country-style home. Here the panels back an inset cabinet.

You can use paneling to add old-fashioned charm to nondescript architecture, or to soften a severe room. Here built-up moldings add shape, depth, and grace to ¼-inch birch plywood panels—and acknowledge the peaked ceiling. White paint makes this paneled room look light and fresh, but you could also add character with grain painting or other faux finishes.

Elegant pilasters link this beautiful paneled wainscoting to cornice and ceiling. Note the nice touch where, in order to accommodate a window, a panel is turned sideways but still topped by the dado. The striped moiré on the walls and changeable silk at the window accentuate the rich glowing grain of the mahogany. The gilded console table completes the formal effect.

The modules of frame-and-panel wall covering can provide a serendipitous well-defined spot for displaying artwork. When the picture shares the proportions of the panel, as in this hallway, a frame-within-a-frame effect appears. The picture rail dado topping the wainscoting provides a non-intrusive way to hang the artwork; a decorative cord dresses it up.

GREAT IDEA

THE SUM OF THE PARTS

Sometimes you can put a little bit of everything into a design with happy results. This Craftsman house needed a facelift, and since budget restrictions precluded anything fancy, the owners opted for some easy cosmetic enhancements with an Oriental flavor.

Walls are simply mahogany plywood butt-joined and finished with tung oil; the teal picture rail is bordered by black enamel quarter-round molding. The wonderful pattern on the ceiling is the result of an inspirational accident—imprints left by Chinese newspaper peeled off still-tacky paint.

PANELING
AND
MOLDING

CHOOSING PANELING

The two main types of paneling are sheet and solid board. Sheet paneling is easier to apply over large, unbroken surfaces because of its dimensions; solid boards, however, are simpler to fit around openings and obstructions.

Sheet paneling

Sheet paneling is a catchall term for wall paneling that comes in large, machine-made panels—most commonly 4 by 8 feet. The two primary types are plywood and hardboard.

PLYWOOD PANELING: Any standard, unfinished plywood sheets may be used. You can also buy plywood with a veneer of nearly any species of hardwood or softwood. Prefinished and vinyl-faced decorative styles are also available, as are resin-coated panels designed for painting. Some panels have surfaces with decorative grooves.

HARDBOARD PANELING: Hardboard paneling is usually less expensive than plywood, but it's also less durable and more subject to warping or moisture damage. The most common surface finishes are imitation wood. Panels embossed with a pattern, such as basket weave, wicker, or louver, are available.

Solid-board paneling

Solid-board paneling is, quite simply, any paneling made up of solid pieces of lumber positioned side by side. It can be milled from hardwood or softwood. Generally, the boards have edges specially milled to overlap or interlock. Board thicknesses range from $\frac{1}{4}$ to $\frac{7}{8}$ inch; widths range from 3 to 12 inches; lengths range from 6 to 20 feet.

LUMBERYARD LINGO

Lumber sizes

Most beginners assume that a 1 by 6 is 1 inch thick by 6 inches wide. It's not. Such numbers give the nominal size of the lumber. When the piece is dried and surfaced (planed), it's reduced to a smaller size. The chart below gives nominal and actual sizes of standard lumber.

Lumber Sizes

NOMINAL SIZE	SURFACE (ACTUAL) SIZE
1 by 2	$\frac{3}{4}$" by 1 $\frac{1}{2}$"
1 by 3	$\frac{3}{4}$" by 2 $\frac{1}{2}$"
1 by 4	$\frac{3}{4}$" by 3 $\frac{1}{2}$"
1 by 6	$\frac{3}{4}$" by 5 $\frac{1}{2}$"
1 by 8	$\frac{3}{4}$" by 7 $\frac{1}{4}$"
1 by 10	$\frac{3}{4}$" by 9 $\frac{1}{4}$"
1 by 12	$\frac{3}{4}$" by 11 $\frac{1}{4}$"

Types of wood

HARDWOOD: Milled from broad-leafed, deciduous trees, such as birch, cherry, mahogany, maple, oak, pecan, rosewood, teak, and walnut. Hardwoods are usually, though not always, more durable than softwoods.

SOFTWOOD: Milled from evergreens (conifers) such as cedar, cypress, fir, hemlock, pine, redwood, and spruce. As a rule, softwoods are easier to tool. The availability and price of softwoods versus hardwoods varies by region.

Lumber grades

Clear softwood paneling boards normally correspond to any formal Select or Finish board grade; knotty panels to Common 2 and 3 grades. Some species, such as redwood and Southern pine, have their own designations. Boards may be surfaced either smooth or resawn (rough).

VERTICAL OR FLAT-GRAIN: Depending on the cut of the millsaw, lumber will have either parallel grain lines running the length of the piece (vertical grain) or a marbled appearance (flat grain). When you can, choose vertical-grain paneling; it's less likely to warp or shrink, and looks better. Some vertical grain lumber commands a premium price.

Moisture content

When wood is sawn, it's still "green"—that is, unseasoned. Before it's ready for use, most lumber is dried, either by air-drying or kiln-drying. To avoid shrinkage and cupping, always look for kiln-dried ("KD") boards.

CHOOSING MOLDING

Traditional wood moldings come in many standard patterns (or profiles) and sizes. You can buy them natural, prefinished (painted or stained), or wrapped with printed vinyl. Lengths range from 3 to 20 feet. They are commonly milled from pine although hardwoods are available, and custom moldings can be made. You can also find plastic, vinyl, or aluminum moldings that look like wood. Many different effects can be made by combining stock molding profiles. A few are pictured at right.

Though decorative, wood moldings are functional, too. They hide cracks on inside corners; protect outside corners; and span gaps between walls and windows, door jambs, and floors.

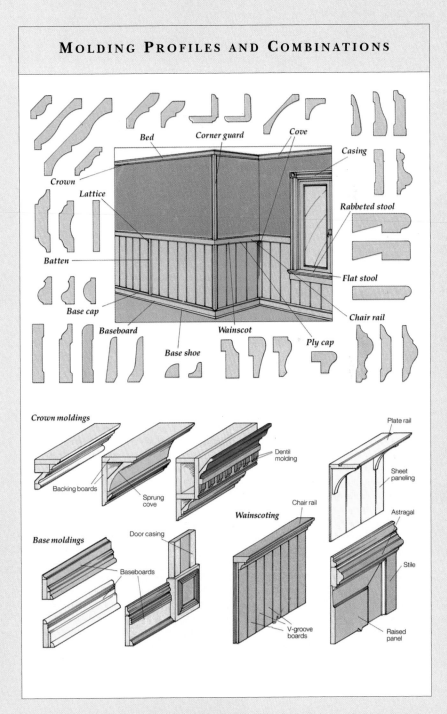

MOLDING PROFILES AND COMBINATIONS

Bed · Corner guard · Cove · Casing · Crown · Lattice · Batten · Base cap · Baseboard · Base shoe · Wainscot · Ply cap · Chair rail · Flat stool · Rabbeted stool

Crown moldings · Backing boards · Sprung cove · Dentil molding · Plate rail · Sheet paneling · Astragal · Stile · Chair rail · Wainscoting · Base moldings · Door casing · Baseboards · V-groove boards · Raised panel

Window Treatments

Window treatments are of immeasurable importance in setting the tone of a room and the options for its design. They can take center stage, boldly focusing attention on themselves, or they can subtly blend with wallcoverings and other furnishings. They can frame or filter natural light—or block it entirely. Some window treatments direct the eye toward lovely outdoor views, while others shield occupants from prying eyes.

When you are deciding what to choose, remember that window treatments are a part of the decor, not an isolated item. Though the options for their design may seem overwhelming, you can focus on your task by learning what the choices are and deciding what you like. Look at pictures; use your imagination; enlist the opinions of friends; get the help of a professional designer if you need it.

Yards and yards of cheesecloth give a contemporary twist to traditional sheers. Here panels of this inexpensive fabric were cut more than twice the rod-to-floor length and each cut end was gathered onto the rod, leaving the midpoints to puddle on the floor in a series of scallops. More cheesecloth was bunched and draped along the rod. A spritz of water crinkled the hanging fabric.

CURTAINS AND DRAPERIES

FOLDS, PLEATS, SWAGS, OR GATHERS of fabric add visual excitement to a window. They soften hard edges, warm cold spaces, and cool hot rooms. They can transform the everyday into the extraordinary—or celebrate simplicity. They can be elaborately structured, festooned with trimmings, tailored, demure, homespun, or delicate. Choose a look that complements your decor, and then design it to be fixed or operable, as suits your needs.

Exquisite curtains finish this stately sitting room with a dignified but lighthearted flourish. Proportion is the key to this successful design: Widely spaced pleats attach to rings; the poles, bows, swagged cord, and tassels are grand—as they should be up near the high ceiling. The holdbacks are raised to provide a full view while the fabric blends quietly with the walls.

Garden rooms call for window treatments that enhance the natural beauty surrounding them. Here soft floral rod-pocket curtains on fabric-covered poles are tied and poufed just below the sill. The curtains are bound with the fabric that covers the poles. Tortoiseshell bamboo shades add texture to the window treatment and complement the rattan furniture.

Rod-pocket curtains with attached shaped valances slide as one over these fluted poles. If you would prefer them to work independently, separate the valances on a second pole. A coordinated line of fabric and wallpaper provides the successful mix of sunny prints, stripes, and borders. Note how the border above the window acts as a valance when the curtains are open.

Opposite: Offbeat semitailored curtains are the perfect choice in this eclectic room. The classically figured outer fabric is completely lined with a subtle stripe. Curtains are cut a little longer than the window to allow for the jaunty fold-over cuff, and a little wider so they fall in soft scallops where fixed to the wall (small rings are pegged to wall by little brass drawer pulls).

A room of refinement deserves a fabulous finish at the windows. At first glance this draped valance with tied-back curtains appears as traditional as could be. A closer look reveals exaggerated proportions and a quirky dagged trim. The color, motif, and scale of the fabric all work beautifully. Notice how the tasseled tiebacks fall at the break in the paneling.

Opposite above: Generous draperies that frame the walk-in bay in this traditionally furnished sitting area can be closed for shade or privacy. Cream and green silk gingham and loose ecru slipcovers give an informal twist to formal furnishings, making the room comfortable and inviting. If these draperies followed the shape of the bay, the mood would be less intimate.

Opposite below: This formal curtain and valance combination goes to great lengths to impart a romantic mood. The deep bell valance crowned with poufs and lined in teal moiré covers stationary panels that puddle luxuriously on the floor. The ruched welt punctuated with a narrow contrasting piping adds body and definition. Coordinating fabric covers the chair and ottoman.

It would be a shame to spoil this light, airy room with heavy, opaque curtains or shades. Instead, tightly gathered sheer curtains fall translucently over a softly scalloped Austrian shade. The sheer fabric picks up a tinge of pale yellow from the walls, and the effect is delightfully delicate. Shirred moiré tiebacks punctuate the treatment, echoing the deep color of the potted greenery.

Opposite: Dressy fabrics with a rich mix of color and pattern are an unexpected choice for a bathroom, but in a large room with old-fashioned fixtures they give just the right touch. Here a luminous striped swag covers a simple cornice box; edge-softening corner tendrils and tiebacks are made from dried flowers. A formal drapery on the tub enhances the exotic mood.

In a nod to its corner setting, this window is trimmed with an asymmetrical swag and cascade. Crisp taffeta hangs in great scrunchy but weightless folds over the delicate hand-embroidered net sheers. The sunny yellow color, whimsical painted flower basket, and overblown rosettes add to the charm of this contemporary twist on tradition.

COMPARING FIBERS

NATURAL FIBERS

COTTON

ADVANTAGES: Cotton is stable and durable, resists moths and abrasion, is nonstatic, and comes in a wide range of weights, textures, and patterns.

DISADVANTAGES: Cotton will fade and rot in the sun and can mildew. Untreated cotton will wrinkle and shrink during cleaning; it will also burn.

LINEN

ADVANTAGES: Strong and durable, linen is nonstatic and resists moths, soil, and sun rot.

DISADVANTAGES: Linen will fade in the sun and will wrinkle unless blended with more stable fibers, such as cotton or polyester. It can also stretch or shrink in humid climates unless blended with such nonabsorbent synthetics as acrylic or polyester. It will also burn unless treated.

SILK

ADVANTAGES: Silk is long lasting if handled carefully. It resists abrasion and moths.

DISADVANTAGES: Silk will fade and rot in the sun. It can mildew, wrinkle, and pick up static electricity. Silk will burn unless treated.

WOOL

ADVANTAGES: A durable fiber, wool is most stable if blended with synthetics.

DISADVANTAGES: Wool will fade and rot in the sun. It also reacts to humidity and temperature changes, picks up static electricity, pills, and must be treated to resist moths and mildew. Wool will burn unless treated.

SYNTHETIC FIBERS

ACETATE

ADVANTAGES: Sunfast when solution-dyed, acetate is stable and resists moths, mildew, and sun rot. It will melt rather than burn.

DISADVANTAGES: Acetate will wrinkle. It's also subject to abrasion and will pick up static electricity.

ACRYLIC

ADVANTAGES: Acrylic, which is stable, durable, and wrinkleproof, also resists moths, mildew, abrasion, and sun rot. Moreover, it has insulating qualities. Acrylic will melt rather than burn.

DISADVANTAGES: Colors may darken slightly in the sun. The fabric picks up static electricity and will pill.

NYLON and

ADVANTAGES: Stable, durable, and wrinkleproof, nylon has insulating qualities and resists abrasion, mildew, moths, soil. It will melt rather than burn.

DISADVANTAGES: Nylon fades and eventually rots in the sun. It also picks up static electricity and will pill.

POLYESTER

ADVANTAGES: Polyester is stable, durable, sunfast, and wrinkleproof. It also resists abrasion, flame, mildew, moths, and sun rot.

DISADVANTAGES: Polyester picks up static electricity and will pill.

RAYON

ADVANTAGES: Rayon resists moths and has insulating qualities.

DISADVANTAGES: Rayon is not stable unless it's treated. It will rot in the sun, mildew, and wrinkle unless blended with a more stable fiber. It's also subject to abrasion. Rayon will burn unless treated.

TOPS AND TRIMS

All that fabric, all those edges—why not finish them with great finesse? There are so many options for drapery trimmings, both ready- and custom-made, that you can create virtually any effect you can dream up. Keep an eye on proportion, and don't let anyone tell you the details don't make a difference—they do.

Simple knots finish the ends of the natty jumbo welting that trims these perky gathered valances. No fuss, no frills. See how the lining fabric matches the window trim.

This festival of color and pattern is full of good ideas: scallops fixed by brass medallions, tasseled cord "tiebacks," two fringes, bold pattern mix, and excellent color balance.

A pretty double border gives a crisp finish to lovely cloud shades. The flat lower layer has a binding of the drapery fabric; the upper is a ruffle of tiny knife pleats accentuated with red piping and the interesting "tassel."

A simple pleated swag valance is a sweet topper for a small window. It works as the only adornment—or it can sit neatly above a shirred organdy café curtain. Rosettes echo the motif of the fabric.

A header must be fully double to gather up on the curtain rod with this full, rounded look. The folds work best with a crisp fabric like chintz, but an interlining can give needed body to a softer weave. The tasseled trim gives a soft finish to the shaped lower edge.

This dagged (zigzag-edged) double ruffle is actually made of hundreds of faille triangles, hemmed individually, overlapped, and gathered. It makes a nod to the antique, but is quite contemporary.

SHADES

FLEXIBILITY IS THE RULE with window shades. By definition, they adjust up or down and can be stopped at any level, so they are an ideal choice when partial coverage is desired. Shades can hang flat, in pleats, poufs, or drapes. They can be made from cloth, paper, woven reed, or any other flexible material. They can be unobtrusive or elaborate, as you wish, and can stand alone or work as part of another treatment.

Cloud shades always give a soft finish to a decor. Their poufed scallops are formed by cords pulled through rings sewn on the reverse side, and they are easy to raise and lower. In this bay, simple shades have shirred headers; the middle one seems to float effortlessly in the arched window.

Stagecoach shades roll to the front to show off the contrasting lining. These, which are a silk variation on the theme, soften the window but are not long enough to provide total privacy. They hook to the rod over neat rosettes, and ombré wire-edged ribbon adds further decorative support.

Simple matchstick shades are the perfect utilitarian choice for a Craftsman
style home, especially as a backdrop to these period light fixtures. The
shades are unobtrusive but attractive. They are inexpensive, readily available, can be cut to size, and transform glaring sunlight into a beautiful
translucent glow. They do not, however, offer nighttime privacy.

WINDOW TREATMENT *Questionnaire*

A quick glance at the questionnaire below can start the ideas flowing. As you develop your plans, come back to this page often; then you'll be sure that you've chosen a treatment that meets as many of your needs as possible.

DESIGN GUIDELINES

- What's the style of your home and its furnishings? Often, it will suggest a window treatment style.
- Is the window distinctive? Perhaps some interesting architectural details deserve emphasis.
- Are the window's proportions pleasing? If not, try a treatment that masks them, such as a tall cornice over a squat window.
- Is the view outstanding? If it is, choose a treatment that won't detract from what's outdoors.
- How much space surrounds the window? Ideally, you should be able to stack treatments off the window. Where space is limited, choose a treatment that stacks compactly.
- How much coverage do you want? Options range from inside mounts to floor-to-ceiling.
- How will your window treatments look from the outside? If your home can be viewed from the street, aim for a consistent look at the windows; it should be in keeping with the exterior style of the house.

PRACTICAL QUESTIONS

- How much privacy do you need? Lace and sheer treatments give some daytime privacy; opaque treatments block the view from outside at night.
- How much natural light do you want inside the room? For maximum light, choose a treatment that, when open, clears the glass.
- Do you need to control glare? Sheer and translucent window treatments cut glare while admitting diffused light.
- Do you need protection against sun damage? A light-diffusing treatment minimizes sun damage. Lining fabric treatments will protect furnishings and fabrics.
- How much ventilation do you want? Where good ventilation is a priority, choose a window treatment that doesn't block the flow of air.
- Is noise control a consideration? Lined fabric treatments muffle sound most effectively.
- Is the window frequently opened and closed? If so, the treatment should not get in the way.
- What's your life-style? If it's hectic, choose durable treatments that are easy to maintain. Save elaborate looks and fancy fabrics for less frequently used rooms.
- What about your current furnishings? If you plan to live with them for a while, choose a window treatment that works with what you have. If you're planning to redecorate, you may be able to install a simple treatment now, such as a valance or blind, and add to it later on when your budget or schedule allows.

CHILD SAFETY

- Are drapery, shade, or blind cords within the reach of babies or young children? Clamp cords to the window treatment itself or wrap them around a cleat mounted high on the wall. Shortened cords and wands are available by special order.
- Can windows be opened enough for a child to fall out? Install window locks that allow only partial opening (but can be easily unlocked in an emergency).
- Can children climb furniture to reach windows? Move furniture away from the windows to put temptation out of reach.
- Can young children easily pull on curtains or draperies? A temporary solution is to loop them up, beyond a child's reach. Also, be sure that mounting hardware is securely fastened to the wall.

SHUTTERS AND BLINDS

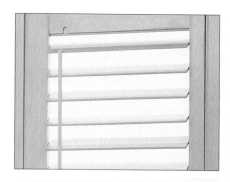

ADJUSTABLE LOUVERS AND VANES give shutters and blinds unique qualities. They can be tilted to filter the light, leveled to reveal the view, or shifted to completely block it. Blinds can be raised so they almost completely disappear. Shutters can be folded against the wall, but may be awkward. Shutters and blinds, available in many styles, give a tailored look, which can be softened when combined with other treatments.

Custom-made shutters are a handsome, tailored choice for this window wall, where a fussier treatment might compete with the view. Note how the upper units hinge at the center to swing under the peak.

Plantation shutters are readily available at home centers. Shutters create a quiet, restful atmosphere and—because you can peek through them—a bit of mystery. Combined with a draped swag that ties them into the arched window, they make a pretty choice.

Blinds are a good choice when you want flexible, unobtrusive door coverings. When desired, light can stream through them—or the vanes can be closed. Horizontal blinds like these can be raised and totally concealed, while blinds with vertical vanes can open like curtains to clear the doors.

If you would like to put a personal touch on a window treatment, but don't want to get involved in a major sewing project, consider jazzing up some shades. Ready-made shades are perfect candidates for added embellishment. If you're a bit more ambitious, flat quilted shades are an easy sewing project.

This window shade serves a dual purpose when it is pulled down: darkening the room and teaching math. You can stencil a design like this onto a plain, ready-made shade with acrylic paints.

A tortoiseshell bamboo shade imparts an Oriental air to a window. When trimmed with black borders and tassels, it becomes elegant. You can easily glue fabric to the self-valance and lower edges, and a few stitches will secure the tassels.

Each of these quilted shades hangs on three rods; the top and middle rods rest in brackets. Lowering the top rods to the middle brackets permits a partial view. If installed so the lower rods moved, you could lift them to create a valance.

SCREENS

SCREENS ARE RIGID FRAMES filled with a translucent material that filters and diffuses light. They may slide, be fixed, or fold accordion-style. Screens can have an inner framework that supports the filler material, which may be plain or patterned. Their unique decorative quality can be as important as that of any other piece of art. We think of screens as being characteristic of Oriental homes, but they can assume many other looks.

ABOUT SHOJI SCREENS

Screens of lace stretched over wood frames fit snugly in the sections of this graceful country Dutch window. The densely figured sheer fabric provides privacy, light, and decoration. A flat, fixed window treatment like this also allows a mirror to be placed above the vanity—something that would be inconvenient and unsightly if in plain view of the street.

Shoji screens typically slide to cover or reveal a window. This one fits right over a conventional aluminum window, and was added when the house was remodeled in an overall Oriental design. The grooved frame is as simple and elegant as the screen it holds.

Opposite: A round window can be difficult to cover without obscuring its shape. One solution is to use a fixed translucent screen, which allows light to enter but assures privacy. The Japanese metalwork that decorates this Shoji screen gives it the importance of a picture. The cedar grille and various textures are pretty against the fabric covered wall.

These custom-made decorative screens consist of wood frames with translucent inserts. Although often found instead of windows in traditional Japanese homes, where deep overhangs protect the screens, elsewhere shojis are typically used as treatments for existing windows.

- Rice paper is the traditional insert material, but because it tears so easily it has been largely supplanted by fiberglass synskin, which has a similar look and texture. Eventually, the fiberglass deteriorates in sunlight and must be replaced. Other synthetic materials, many of which come from Japan, are also used.
- Shoji screens can be made to slide along a wood track or fold over a window like shutters. Several panels can be hinged together and stacked at one side of the window. Shoji screens can be used for doorways as well as windows; they are also appropriate as room dividers.
- The screens are comparably priced to custom wood shutters.

Flooring and Floor Covering

Flooring is a structural component of your home; it can be altered, but not as easily as wall covering. Flooring also has to work — it gets walked on, spilled on, rolled across, and washed. And, it contributes more to the character of a room than most of us at first recognize, so it is wise to think about your floors early in any decorating project. Luckily, there are plenty of great-looking options that create different effects, solve different problems, and suit many budgets.

Because flooring is laid from component pieces, it is easier than you might at first think to create a unique effect. Allover or border checkerboard and stripe patterns are obvious choices, but many other straight-edged patterns are easy to compose. Ceramic tiles come in a variety of shapes, other materials can be cut to order. Alternatively, you can add pattern to a wood floor with paint or stain, or as shown above, you can even mix materials.

Polished hardwood adds a glowing finish to a room. Here, a floating floor system of veneer strips atop tongue-and-groove backing boards leads the eye down a dressing area corridor. The handsome storage wall and vanity cabinets are made of cedar.

WOOD

WOOD IS A TRADITIONAL FLOORING appropriate to many styles of architecture. It can be clear finished, stained, pickled, bleached, or painted; these treatments vary in durability and maintenance requirements. Depending upon the species of tree and the style of board used, a remarkable variety of looks is available. Some of these are characteristic of particular period styles—so do some research to determine what is right for you.

Below left: Porch and deck paint offers a fairly durable surface for floors that don't get too much rugged traffic. The floor in this wonderful studio-in-the-clouds is painted sky blue. The effect is just what this artist wanted—it would also work well for a sunroom, bedroom, or family room. Also consider paint as a short-term fix for damaged floors that you are not ready to completely redo.

Below right: Square columns form a curved passageway through this room, which is part of a guest suite. At the base of each column the classic oak strip floor has been accented with small squares stained through a stencil. Note how the various squares and rectangles used in the room form a subtle background of squares and rectangles for the curved passageway.

PAINTED DECORATION

Often a room looks undecorated and cold if the floors are plain and bare, so carpets are used to complete and soften the look. Throughout history paint has been used to imitate decorative woven carpeting—paint is relatively inexpensive and many effects are easily achievable by careful amateurs.

For a romantically old-fashioned look, an old strip floor was washed with white paint, stenciled with flowers and butterflies in the field and stripes and checks around the edges. Then it was sealed with a clear finish.

Opposite above: In this classic Georgian entry hallway the plank floor was painted in a bold black and gold checkerboard. This is an easy design to duplicate: Paint the floor gold first; then use tape to mask alternate squares, and paint with black.

Opposite below: The floor in the eating area of this country kitchen has been painted in imitation of a painted floorcloth—which in turn would have imitated a woven rug. A combing tool was used to paint the stripes.

CARPETS AND RUGS

A SOFT SURFACE UNDERFOOT is always welcoming. For this reason, and because it absorbs sound, carpeting is a popular choice for bedroom, living room, and hall floors. Carpeting is also a great way to bring color and pattern into your decor. It comes in many fibers and textures, with price and maintenance varying as well. Technically, carpets are attached and rugs loose; however, Oriental rugs are often referred to as carpets.

Left: Oriental carpets look wonderful in almost any decor. They come in myriad colors and patterns—geometric or floral, realistic or stylized—and in all sizes and price ranges. An Oriental carpet can provide focus or background to a room's design. Here a small antique carpet anchors smart modern furniture.

Right: A multihued geometric rug makes a bold transition between the upholstered chair and golden-oak strip flooring. Carpet retailers can often seam diverse edging and field components into one custom covering. Many lines of carpeting include coordinating borders.

Opposite: Luxurious wall-to-wall carpeting is soft, soothing, and quiet. This bedroom is a cocoon of ecru mottled with lavender; everything about it promises a gentle repose. Note that the louvered shutters give an unfussy finish to the windows while softly filtering the daylight.

RESILIENT FLOORING

IF YOU THINK ALL RESILIENT GOODS have a hard-times aura about them, think again: the selection of materials, colors, patterns, and textures is inspiring. Made from solid vinyl, rubber, or polyurethane, this flooring is the easiest and usually least expensive form to install. It is available in tiles or sheets. For those who want a true midcentury look, traditional linoleum is making a comeback.

Opposite left: If you think creatively, you can design a distinctive floor with plain vinyl tiles. Here, black flooring inset with turquoise diamonds accents a narrow kitchen. Sleek, pale gray cabinets and white tiled and mirrored walls add light; the dark floor and countertops add a sophisticated finish.

Opposite right: Resilient flooring is available in any number of fanciful and realistic patterns. You might assume that this country kitchen has a flagstone floor—and that is exactly what the owners desired. But this one, of resilient sheet goods, is low-maintenance, easy on the feet, and much less expensive to install.

Alternating gray and white vinyl tiles form an easy-to-live-with kitchen floor. When placed diagonally they make a room look larger. Here they enliven a small, nearly all-white kitchen without overpowering it. Self-adhesive tiles are available for the do-it-yourselfer.

CERAMIC AND STONE TILE

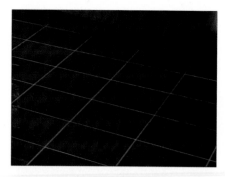

FOR VARIETY AND DURABILITY, you couldn't do better than select a stone or ceramic tile floor. Glazed tile and properly sealed terra-cotta and stone are impervious and offer endless choices for working colorful pattern into a room—but can be cold or slippery, and taxing to stand on. As with wood, certain types of tile and stone are characteristic of specific architectural styles; they can be striking in a contemporary home.

Rustic terra-cotta tiles make an informal but beautiful floor. Shown here in a Southwestern home, they are also characteristic of Mediterranean architecture. They are available glazed and unglazed, and in many shapes, sizes, colors, and patterns. They are heavy and require a sturdy subfloor.

Simple white glazed ceramic tiles set with a diagonal self-border impart a special finish to this pretty bathroom. A detail of this sort, which can be done with contrasting as well as matching tiles, is an easy and usually inexpensive way to dress up a floor.

Opposite: Polished black granite tiles are virtually indestructible, and a perfect choice for a sophisticated kitchen, bath or foyer. Butted edge-to-edge here, they create a smooth, gleaming expanse that complements the sleek curving cabinetry and the appliances.

A checkerboard floor and striped wainscoting of polished marble tiles create an unexpected setting for this whimsical basin. The bright diamonds embedded in the floor are fiber optic lights; these are a nice touch for a powder room where users may be unfamiliar with the layout.

Opposite above: A room with grand proportions can support a visually weighty floor. Irregular flagstones add random color, pattern, and texture that contrast with the bold grid of the open ceiling and the tailored cabinets. Flagstone also comes in uniform tiles, which give a more sedate look.

Opposite below: Large rectangular stone slabs echo the custom steel windows at the end of this corridor. They are not polished; their surface is slightly irregular, and their color is gently variegated. In the light falling through the windows they become a marvelous carpet of subtle tones. The floor continues as an exterior walkway.

FLOORING MATERIALS

Flooring is of course an essential part of your house; it finishes the structure and the decor. It can be changed, but doing so is sometimes costly and labor-intensive. When choosing flooring, consider its practical as well as aesthetic qualities—you'll want to enjoy living with it, as well as looking at it.

RESILIENT FLOORING

ADVANTAGES: Generally made from solid vinyl, polyurethane, or rubber, resilients are moisture- and stain-resistant, flexible, easy to install, and simple to maintain. They are comfortable underfoot. The variety of colors, textures, patterns, and styles is virtually endless. Tiles can be mixed to form custom patterns or provide color accents.

• Resilients are good for do-it-your-self projects; tiles are easier to lay than sheet goods. Sheets run up to 12 feet wide, allowing seamless floors in small rooms; tiles are generally 12 inches square.

DISADVANTAGES: Resilients are relatively soft, so are vulnerable to dents and tears; sometimes such damage can be repaired. Tiles may collect moisture between seams if improperly installed.

COST: Prices (uninstalled) range from about $1.50 a square foot for the least expensive tile to nearly $15. Sheet vinyls range from about 35 cents to $5.50 a square foot. Vinyl is least expensive. Expect to pay a premium for custom tiles and for imported products.

CERAMIC TILE

ADVANTAGES: Made from hard-fired slabs of clay, ceramic tile is available in dozens of patterns, colors, shapes, and finishes. It is durable, easy to maintain, and attractive. Tiles are usually classified as *quarry tile,* unglazed red-clay tiles that are rough and water-resistant; *pavers,* rugged unglazed tiles in earth tones; and *glazed tile,* available in many colors in glossy, matte, or textured finishes.

• Tile sizes run a gamut of widths, lengths, and thicknesses. By mixing sizes and colors, creative tile workers can fashion a wide range of border treatments and field accents.

DISADVANTAGES: Tile can be cold, noisy, and if glazed, slippery underfoot. If not properly grouted, tiles can leak moisture; some tiles will stain unless properly sealed. Grout spaces can be tough to keep clean.

COST: Tile can cost from about $1 per square foot to nearly $40, uninstalled. Those with three-dimensional patterns and multicolored glazes can easily cost double. Purer clays fired at higher temperatures generally make costlier but better-wearing tiles.

STONE

ADVANTAGES: Natural stone (such as slate, flagstone, marble, granite, and limestone) has been used as flooring for centuries. Today, its use is even more practical, thanks to the development of sealers and finishes. Easy to maintain, masonry flooring is also virtually indestructible. Stone can be used in its natural shape or cut into uniform pieces—rectangular blocks or more formal tiles. Generally, uniform pieces are butted tightly together; irregular flagstone requires grouted joints. Man-made masonry products, specifically heat-retaining brick, are also an option for indoor use. Even colored or textured concrete can be used for finish flooring.

DISADVANTAGES: The cost of most masonry flooring is high. Moreover, the weight of the materials requires a very strong, well-supported subfloor. Some stone—marble in particular—is cold and slippery underfoot. Careful sealing is a must; certain stones, such as limestone or marble, absorb stains and dirt readily.

COST: From $3 per square foot for slate to $30 and over for granite.

WOOD

ADVANTAGES: A classic hardwood floor creates a warm decor, feels good underfoot, and can be refinished. Oak is most common; maple, birch, cherry, and beech are also available. Softwood (pine) is appropriate for some country or reproduction homes; it dents and scratches easily, but has character.

- The three basic types are *strip,* narrow tongue-and-groove boards in random lengths; *planks,* tongue-and-groove boards in various widths and random lengths; and *wood tile,* often patterned in parquet fashion. "Floating" floor systems have several veneered strips atop each tongue-and-groove backing board.
- Wood flooring may be factory-prefinished or unfinished, so that it can be sanded and finished in place. Most floors can be refinished; floating systems cannot.

DISADVANTAGES: Moisture and inadequate floor substructure can be problematic. Some finishes scratch easily. Bleaching and some staining processes may wear unevenly and are difficult to repair.

COST: From $7.50 to $13 per square foot, installed, depending on type, quality, and finish. Floating systems are generally most expensive.

CARPETING

ADVANTAGES: Carpeting cushions feet, provides firm traction, and helps deaden sound. It's especially useful to define areas in multiuse layouts or master suites. New tightly woven commercial products are making carpeting a more practical option.

DISADVANTAGES: Generally, the more elaborate the material and weave, the greater the problems from moisture absorption, staining, and mildew. Carpeting used in bathrooms should be short-pile and unsculptured. Woven or loop-pile wool should be confined to dressing areas. Nylon and other synthetic carpets are a better choice for splash zones; these are washable and hold up well in moist conditions.

COST: Like resilient flooring, carpeting is available in an array of styles and materials at many prices.

PART 3

Room by Room

Living Spaces

D ecorating living and dining areas is in many ways a challenge. These are the public parts of our homes, places where we welcome friends as well as family. We want these areas to reflect something of our character, perhaps to showcase some special interest or

unique talent, and to be inviting—but not to reveal our more intimate habits. At the same time, we want them to be comfortable for everyday living.

In this chapter you'll find formal, informal, and eclectic decorating ideas for living rooms, dining rooms, and libraries. There is help for integrating electronic equipment with your decor, and for planning shelves. There are also some great ideas for making the most of small spaces—the nooks and crannies that can provide a quiet and relaxing retreat from the world at large.

"A New York loft" was the dream of a California homeowner who commissioned this multilevel, multipurpose room, which features successfully defined living areas yet has no dividing walls. The space is not as grand as you might at first think, but the soaring ceiling and thoughtfully detailed but simple decor give it a gracious air.

LIVING ROOMS

THE WAY YOU FURNISH YOUR LIVING ROOM depends not only upon your taste but also on the way the space is used. Do you use your living room every day? For dining? Working? During the day? Do children use it? Is there an exterior door that opens into it? Do you have a television, sound system, or even a telephone there? Answers to these questions will help set parameters for furnishings, flooring, and electrical support.

Although quite small, the living room in this urban condominium appears striking and dramatic by virtue of its architecture—large windows, recessed floor, and raised ceiling all have strong rectilinear frames. The Oriental carpet and rich color scheme lend a venerable air to the very contemporary furnishings.

An interesting array of textures sets the stage in this room. The soft, matte finish of brick, wood paneling and ceiling, and carpeting are contrasted by the glass wall and tabletop; plump leather sofas have a subtle sheen. The coffee table is an arresting and graphic focal point—as much sculpture as furniture.

Translucent windows, cinderblock walls, and parquet floor give this room a textured shell that would fight complicated furnishings. But sleek, simple shapes in a limited palette decorate it with comfortable ease. A few carefully chosen accessories impart an exotic air to the room.

At once formal and comfortable, this room combines hushed hues and refined patterns with neoclassical motifs for an understated elegance. The glazed, sponged walls and ceiling create an ethereal background; the monochromatic palette is broken only by the greens and flowers.

This towering steel book wall serves as a focal point in a large contemporary living room; the shelves are so sturdy that they can be climbed like a ladder. Light pouring through the window wall bounces off steel shelves, piano, tailored leather sofa, glass-topped coffee table, and polished floor to fill the room with a soft, rich glow.

A fireplace provides a welcome focus to any living room, but too often you must choose between a view of the flames or the great outdoors. Windows around the massive stone hearth solve the problem in this room, which is furnished in a comfortable formal country style.

This creamy living room is home to a collection of sculpture and ceramics. The sectional sofa is inviting, yet blends with the walls and carpet to show off the artwork. The minimalist fireplace, surrounded by a huge slab of marble, is flanked by mirrored niches that have a windowlike effect as they reflect the collection, the shutters, and a landscape painting.

SHELVING AND MEDIA CABINETRY

When planning shelves and cabinetry for electronic equipment, the time you spend measuring and calculating is time well spent. The illustrations will help you to determine shelf height.

Here are some other points to keep in mind.

- Calculate shelving in linear, not square, feet.
- Adjustable shelves offer the most flexibility.
- Plan adequately for the weight of books, electronic equipment, and collectibles.

- Place media equipment where it will be easy to use or view.
- Place heavier books on lower shelves.
- Small items such as tapes and compact disks are best stored in drawers.
- Refer to manufacturers' manuals for installation specifications.

IDEAL SHELVING DIMENSIONS

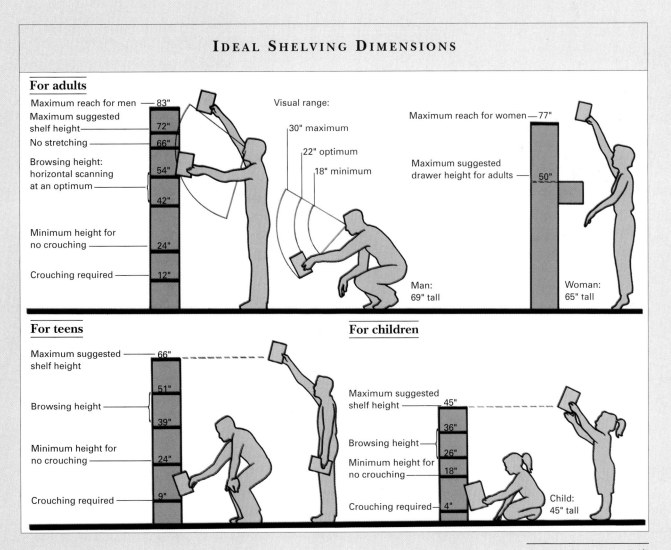

For adults

Maximum reach for men — 83"
Maximum suggested shelf height — 72"
No stretching — 66"
Browsing height: horizontal scanning at an optimum — 54"
42"
Minimum height for no crouching — 24"
Crouching required — 12"

Visual range:
30" maximum
22" optimum
18" minimum

Maximum reach for women — 77"
Maximum suggested drawer height for adults — 50"

Man: 69" tall
Woman: 65" tall

For teens

Maximum suggested shelf height — 66"
51"
Browsing height — 39"
Minimum height for no crouching — 24"
Crouching required — 9"

For children

Maximum suggested shelf height — 45"
36"
Browsing height — 26"
Minimum height for no crouching — 18"
Crouching required — 4"

Child: 45" tall

MEDIA CENTERS

Life today is somehow filled with electronic equipment—sound and video systems that require strategic placement and electrical support. Some people don't mind this gear as part of their decor. If you prefer it hidden, adapt one of these ideas.

This well-designed cabinetry would work as well in a living room, office, or library as it does in this bedroom. The cabinet at the end of the bed houses a projector unit.

Opposite the projector, the retractable screen drops from a floating soffit. Such housing must be custom-made, but it solves the problem in a handsome manner.

A built-in media center, its clear-finished maple doors blending beautifully with the steel-troweled plaster hearth, hides in a corner of this room. When you open the retractable doors the electronic equipment appears.

Here the doors are ajar. Careful mathematics go into the design of such a precisely aligned system.

Armoires suitable for housing electronic equipment are available in a variety of styles. This leather-covered unit would be an asset in any contemporary room.

When open, you see that it houses a well-lighted and fully wired office as well as stereo and pivot-out television. The chair stores inside when the armoire is closed.

Traditional cabinetry can be adapted to hold a swiveling TV. Here a frame-and-panel door retracts horizontally, and a shelf with a turntable pulls out.

LIBRARIES AND RETREATS

LUCKY ARE THOSE who have a room to dedicate to reading, game playing, or even fly-tying. If you do, seize the opportunity to make it not only comfortable, but personable, and furnish it to suit your ideal of library, pool hall, or family room. Whether your sanctuary is private or shared, you can furnish it with traditional accoutrements or eccentric accessories, as befits the way you'll use it.

Glass-door library cases form a traditional backdrop in a tailored library, and protect books from dust. These shelves are recessed so the doors swing out over a counter so as not to bump book searchers. In keeping with the formal cabinetry, a leather-topped table with a candlestick lamp serves as a desk for reading or correspondence.

Opposite: Thoughts of a classic library call up images of nineteenth century elegance, with commodious wing chairs, table lamps, rich, dark-toned wood and books, books, books. This library is fitted with handsome, finely detailed paneling that surrounds the books, concealing the shelf support system. The brass tubes above the shelves hold miniature lights. Chairs and side table invite one to read or linger over a cup of tea.

A pool table is likely to dominate any room it inhabits, and this one is no exception. Shelves line one wall, providing space for books, trophies, photos, and other memorabilia. Dignified but comfortable chairs are set for observation or conversation. The checkered pendant light is fun, but not too—there is serious business to transact here.

Some people have no need for a real library, or a home office, or even a studio, but even so they may have a pastime so important that it warrants a dedicated room. In this case, fly-fishing rules, with all available surfaces devoted to practical or sentimental gear. The space over the built-in closet provides additional storage for important and hard-to-stow items.

This small, interesting library features concrete and stone walls. The curved wall is lined with floating maple shelves. The velvet sofa echoes the texture and color of the walls, yet promises a soft read. The mood here is cool, subdued, and rather serious.

Even if you lack the space to devote an entire room to a library, you may be able to set up a good substitute in an alcove such as this, where bench seating lines two walls and shelves over cupboards face a third. Note the shallow counter that extends behind the benches.

BOOK-SHELVES

If you have a lot of books, bookshelves become an important part of your decor. Whether you are incorporating shelves into a new or existing room, ask yourself three questions: What style of shelving is desired? What sizes of books will be stored? How much space is needed to hold the books?

This very simple, very handsome, wall-hung bookcase includes storage niches, drawers, and a desk complete with a pencil groove. Adapt this in bright colors (at a suitable height) for a child's room.

Not everyone requires extensive bookshelves—sometimes all that is called for is a few simple wall-hung boards. This system redefines the classic bracket-and-board system with unpeeled hickory uprights and brackets.

A U-shaped bookcase creates a transitional hallway between an office and adjacent living space. Note that no attempt was made to utilize the traditionally troublesome space in the corners.

Who says a bookcase has to be placed against a wall? Hinged units double as doors, providing entry to "secret" rooms while maximizing storage options. Sliding cases are another possibility.

This custom oak wall unit blends Craftsman-style detailing with clever hinged doors that fold down to rest on narrow open drawers.

Just give this tilted case a pull and it will follow you to a comfortable chair. The jaunty slant allows easier movement and keeps the books from falling over.

DINING AREAS

DINING AREAS may be formal or informal, separate rooms or part of a kitchen or living area. The quality and quantity of natural and artificial light are very influential in a dining area, so as you decorate, consider not only the furnishing style that complements your needs, but also the times of day that you will sit in the room. If your home has more than one place to take a meal, you can create a different ambience in each.

The sleek table and chairs tucked at the end of this kitchen counter share nothing but function with a classic breakfast nook—and function they do. The tabletop is roughly diamond-shaped and will seat three in a pinch. Note the pull-out toaster set into the wall, and the outlet set conveniently below the countertop.

The austere simplicity of this dining room successfully balances rather large furnishings in a fairly small space. The elegant black chairs and accessories stand out against the neutral walls and natural wood floors, beams, and trim. The peaked ceiling makes the room seem more spacious; the view is the most important accessory.

Opposite: The dining area in this great room offers an invitation to more than gracious meals. Diners can enjoy a cheery blaze in the fireplace, or catch the news. Bright colors accent the happy geometry of the spare furnishings; the wall unit provides display and storage. Note that the chair arms slide under the table when not in use.

A traditional multileaved table flanked by formal chairs offers a comfortable and flexible dining place. By day, this pretty room is filled with sunlight. In the evening it assumes a cozy elegance as sconces and candles cast a soft light on the sponged walls and beamed ceiling.

Gardenside dining is an all-weather pleasure in a sunroom. Placing the table next to a window seat saves room and enhances the view. Tapestry-patterned cushions and borders combine with mullioned windows and spring green trim to make this a particularly pleasant spot.

You can always pull one more chair up to a round pedestal table, which offers maximum surface with minimum intrusion in a small area. Here, the clever storage wall on the left features pivoting doors and houses closets, desk, television, ovens, and refrigerator. The attractive shoulder-high cupboard wall masks the rest of the kitchen.

SUNROOMS

Providing light, views, and often fresh air, a sunroom is a transitional zone between a home's interior and garden. These rooms are more window than wall, so the world outside is the dominant accessory—furnishings can be simple; garden furniture and sun-loving plants are always appropriate.

Enclosing a porch or patio is an easy way to create a sunroom. Coordinated furniture and a two-color palette keep this narrow space from looking crowded.

This sunroom has sliding roof panels and handsome fir doors. It doubles as an expanded entryway and a dining nook. The only accessory is a large potted tree.

You need not live in a period house to enjoy a formal conservatory. This English sunroom was prefabricated in Europe. Lacy wrought iron furnishings complement its structural framework.

Use a standard garage door to bring the feeling of a sunroom to a space that has only one exterior wall. This room has a great view and lots of fresh air without the heat that can come with a glass roof.

NOOKS AND CRANNIES

WHILE LIVING SPACES are meant to be social places, there is no denying that most of us yearn for a spot that offers comfortable solitude. Sometimes such nooks and crannies are part of a home's architecture; sometimes you have to create them. But as these photos show, it is well worth the effort to set up a sheltered, private area. Part of the fun is the opportunity to design a vignette that appears inviting from within or without.

No retreat could be easier to create—or more inviting —than a cushion-tossed daybed tucked under corner shelves. This one, topped with pillows dressed in woven ethnic covers, has a casual but tailored appearance; there are storage units beneath and at the end. The massive shelves are actually hollow units that slide over steel rods extending from the wall studs.

Nooks and crannies can be added where they don't exist. This small study nests in a pop-out added to a bedroom. An interesting knee-wall archway gives a sense of privacy while allowing light to pass through. You could create a similar effect in an L-shaped room. The adjacent windows in the corner provide an expanded view from either chair.

An alcove is a natural refuge. This one has grand proportions which are fittingly dressed with classic—and very graceful—draperies and a generous overstuffed armchair. The color scheme is rich and sophisticated, with softly mottled walls topped by a painted border. An impressive crown molding frames the space; darker fabrics frame the view.

Above right: Tuck a window seat between book walls and tuck yourself in for a good read—or daydream over the view. This space at the end of a balcony landing is architecturally pleasant, but uncomplicated—it takes a lot of its character from the bright, boldly patterned textiles that contrast with the buff walls and natural wood tones.

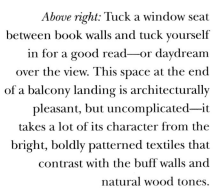

Right: A desk in a corner by a pretty window offers an invitation to reverie and is a great spot for journal keeping or letter writing. The mirror, placed perpendicular to the window, expands the view. The floral fabric chosen for this window shade gives a decidedly feminine air to the decor. With another fabric, the effect could be markedly different.

LIGHTING OPTIONS

Proper lighting, carefully sited and controlled by dimmers, does a lot to make living and dining areas comfortable. But proper doesn't have to mean mundane—or fancy. Here are some clever ideas that add character and enhance ambience.

These whimsical fixtures are just bulbs suspended from ceiling boxes via standard electrical conduit painted black. The fireproof paper shades, secured by interlaced branches, give them character.

Wanting to light their home with candles, and knowing it would be impractical, these homeowners used white paint to transform a grouping of tacky junkyard chandeliers.

A classic Spanish-style chandelier is a natural for this Southwestern dining room. Beeswax sleeves give a sophisticated finish to the candlestick bulbs and conceal the wiring.

This inventive chandelier, fashioned from clamp lights hard-wired into overhead junction boxes, forms the perfect counterpoint for a parking lot mirror and a display of car emblems.

The lighting in this study was designed to look soft in contrast to the concrete wall. A low-voltage cable system follows the wall; louvers control light spill and add style.

Yes, it is a skylight—but the natural light is supplemented by quartz wall washers tucked into the well to bounce off the walls and floor, giving a warm glow to the serene space.

Working Spaces

The nature of the business you pursue sets the basic parameters for office style, but one of the advantages of working at home is that your office can be truly custom-tailored. Some people relish the escape from the corporate environment; others exult in their private executive domain. And of course, not all workspaces are offices—many are studios or workshops. Nor are all home offices income-producing—yours may be for household organization and correspondence. Whatever your situation may be, list the features you'd like to include, be sure to plan carefully for

your electronic needs, and give serious thought to the aesthetics.

For most home-based workers, peace and quiet in a well-lighted space are the keys to a work place that is pleasant and promotes productivity—others thrive without the peace and quiet. Whether your office is a suite, single room, or corner, be sure it works for you.

Book-lined walls frame an archway entry to this office, setting it apart from the rest of the house. The furnishings are spare but comfortable; a rolling chair faces the desk-counter running under the windows, and an easy chair waits for reading. Mini-blinds maintain the clean lines of the window when raised, and the patterned carpet softens the mood. An effective file shelf is tucked under the desk.

THE EXECUTIVE AT HOME

THE DISTRACTIONS of your personal life can make working at home less than easy. While you may enjoy the short commute, you should be in a productive environment when you reach your desk, so set it up professionally. Be sure that chairs and workstations are comfortable, that storage is adequate, and that you can't trip over wires. If you meet with clients in your home, you want them to take you seriously.

If you work closely with another person in your home, one shared office may feel less cramped than two private ones. This elegant room is fitted for partnership. There are two oak desks for individual work, and a comfortable sitting area with a fireplace for conferences. An undercounter refrigerator, computer, plus audio and security gear are housed discreetly in trim cabinetry along one wall.

Opposite: A formal study sets the mood for discussion and problem-solving, making it clear that this home office is a place of business. It is handsomely appointed with a walnut desk and exotic side chairs—the accessories hint at time spent in faraway lands. Shutters at the window can be adjusted to minimize glare—important for making clients feel comfortable.

A desk and credenza may seem corporate, but they leave no doubt that your office is home to a professional. These beautiful custom cabinets are faced with purple-heart and ebony. The curved return helps to define the private work area without erecting a barrier.

If you do not need to close yourself into your office, consider setting up workspace in a common area—a foyer, large hallway, or landing. This desk placed outside a master bedroom is completely professional and suits the night-owl habits of a writer who likes to work when others sleep. Soft colors enhance the quiet mood.

A home office need not be grand to be professional. This U-shaped config-
uration works well in a smaller room, providing storage, workstation, and
conference space all within an easy roll of the chair. While this laminate
system was custom-made, you could assemble a similar setup from readily
available modular units.

FOR DESIGNERS, READERS, AND WRITERS

HOME OFFICES are not for corporate-style business only. If you are a writer, designer, teacher, or avid reader, you will want a workspace that reflects your style and suits the nature of your work. You may prefer a private sanctuary, or need an atelier where colleagues and clients can brainstorm. Perhaps you'd like an informal ambience. Analyze your needs and give them a personal interpretation—you're the boss.

A conference area is central to an architect's or interior designer's workspace. This basement room sports walls sponged to look sunsplashed, the illusion heightened by a halogen bounce-light. Trendy furnishings make an important statement about the type of work done here. An oval pedestal table seats a group comfortably.

A brash yellow wire rack tames office clutter but keeps important reference material handy. In a design-oriented business, choice of accessories is more than usually critical for establishing the proper image.

One half of a two-story addition, this downstairs design office provides plenty of elbow room in the form of twin U-shaped layouts. The overhanging counter, which invites colleagues or clients to pull up for a close look, is wire-mesh safety glass joined to laminated layers of maple plywood; frames are steel. Note the well-designed wall-mounted storage unit.

The adjacent file room features banks of recessed cabinets, ample counter space, and a little corner cubby by the files. Sturdy bookshelves are suspended on industrial threaded rods and steel U-channels.

If you want to integrate your daily life with your work, consider setting up shop in the dining room—or elsewhere with common household furnishings—to make you forget corporate stress. Here an antique plank dining table doubles as work surface and conference center; a pine wardrobe houses office supplies and fax; and a roll-top desk completes the homey atmosphere.

The young, or young-at-heart, may find study or work is less onerous in a cutting-edge comic-book world. This one-wall office meshes industrial with extraterrestrial; it may be the perfect setting for computer-based intellectual exercise. Adjustable plastic shelves fastened to commercial steel U-channels provide a place for everything.

PLANNING AN OFFICE LAYOUT

Your office should be efficient, yet it should also be comfortable for you, your colleagues, and any clients who may visit you. The size and location of the desk—and computer workstation, if different—are critical, so begin your design by locating them in the room and then arrange the other furnishings around them. Be sure to allow sufficient space for and next to electronic equipment. Refer to A Look At Ergonomics on pages 178–179 and the Office Questionnaire on page 187. Then study the floor plans at right as you design your home office layout.

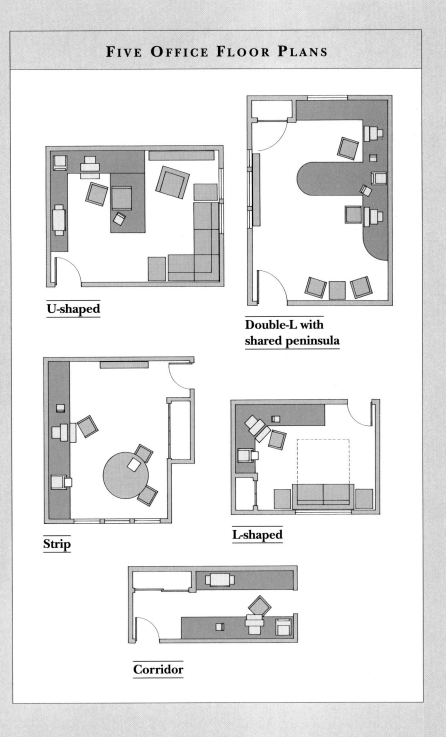

FIVE OFFICE FLOOR PLANS

U-shaped

Double-L with shared peninsula

Strip

L-shaped

Corridor

Opposite: Counter space and book space were what one computer pioneer demanded of his upstairs office. The long, corridor-style layout has continuous counter-tops on one side and floor-to-ceiling bookcases on the other. Wall cases above the window maximize soffit space and house task lights. The window sill is raised for more book space. The corner desk gives extra depth to accommodate the monitor.

Right: A thoughtfully finished basement room can be a comfortable retreat for reading, writing, or contemplation. Beautiful wood built-ins oriented to the wall at playful angles offer a plethora of pullouts and cubbyholes. For the right tasks, a pillow-backed bench is a relaxing alternative to the desk.

Below: Back-to-back desks make a two-person correspondence center fit into a corridor. This one has a traditional library demeanor, with glass-fronted bookcases, gleaming woodwork, and leather chairs. Beyond, a shelf-flanked Palladian window beckons.

A LOOK AT ERGONOMICS

The term ergonomics refers to human engineering—that is, designing equipment, furniture, and workspaces to be both efficient and comfortable for human use. Until recently, little attention was paid to such concerns. But as computer use increased, workers spending long hours at terminals began to show signs of physical strain that had never before been associated with desk work. Frequent complaints of backaches, headaches, neck and shoulder tension, wrist and hand injuries, eyestrain, and general irritability led to the emergence of the ergonomics design field.

SETTING UP YOUR OFFICE

The findings of ergonomists, some of which are discussed below and illustrated on the facing page, are helpful when setting up a home office. But regardless of the furnishings, experts agree that you have to meet them halfway. Yes, your mother was right—Sit up straight and take breaks! Most experts believe that one of the major causes of repetitive stress injuries is the computer's ability to mesmerize.

Desk

As a general starting point, the surface used for writing and other paperwork should be about 28 $\frac{1}{2}$ inches from the floor. However, for comfort, a keyboard surface should stand lower—about 24 to 27 inches high. More important than absolute heights are the body angles and stresses that are induced by the interrelated heights of the keyboard, computer monitor, and chair. You may wish to have both a conventional desk and a computer workstation.

Keyboard

You should be able to type with both arms relaxed at your sides, forearms at right angles to your body, and wrists in a neutral position. The keyboard angle should be neutral (as shown) or, according to some studies, at a slightly negative angle.
- An articulating keyboard tray (AKT) can be positioned at any height and at any distance from the desk edge or computer screen; use this or a simpler pull-out tray to retrofit a too-high surface.
- If you use a pullout keyboard tray, make sure it can hold the mouse, too, so you won't have to constantly reach up to the top of the desk.
- Wristrests, available for both keyboard and mouse use, help guide your position, but you shouldn't press down on them while working.

Chair

Choosing a desk chair is especially important, since you're likely to spend a lot of time in one. A chair with adjustable seat height will allow you to type efficiently as well as work comfortably at your desk. Armrests should be adjustable and should not prevent you from pulling close into your desk or keyboard.
- In good chairs you can change the cant of the seat to produce the most favorable hip-to-knee alignment. Support for your lumbar (lower spine) area is also important, so make sure that the chair firmly fits the small of your back. If necessary, use an adjustable footrest to keep your feet flat on the floor.

Your eyesight

To protect against eyestrain, a computer monitor should be located about 16 to 28 inches (or an arm's length) from the operator's face. Place the top of the monitor even with the top of your head, so that your eyes are aligned with the first few lines on the screen. (One exception: bifocal wearers should align the screen with their line of focus.) A copyholder or slantboard should be positioned at about the same distance as the monitor, slightly to one side or directly below.

- Another source of eyestrain is the balance between light levels in the room and on your monitor. Adjust your screen illumination to match room lighting and turn the contrast up.

- Glare is another big problem. It can come from overhead fixtures, a nearby task lamp, highly reflective surfaces, or a window in front of or behind you. If possible, place yourself at a 90-degree angle to a window or other bright light source. Screen shade or glare guards can help shield your monitor.

Get comfortable

Although it's hard to accomplish, aim to place everything you need on a regular basis within arm's reach. If that's too tough, consider setting up multiple use areas and rolling your chair from zone to zone as required.

- A telephone headset helps relieve the stress of heavy phone use, especially while you're straining to find or do something else.

- Ergonomists recommend looking away from the computer screen and blinking hard at frequent intervals, getting up and stretching every 30 minutes, and taking a break each hour.

- Change your position frequently and plan your time so you can mix tasks. If you need a reminder, you can find several software programs that will prompt you to relax at prescribed intervals—and even guide you through a refreshing exercise break. Or set the alarm on your computer to prompt you from time to time.

Shopping for health

Besides adjustable workstations and ergonomic chairs, look for articulating keyboard trays, monitor lifts, slantboards, adjustable keyboards, trackballs, wristrests, footrests, and headsets. But remember that so-called "ergonomic" products aren't certified. So shop from reputable sources and always ask to test any product before buying it.

AN ERGONOMIC OVERVIEW

Monitor at eye level or slightly lower

Viewing distance 16"–28"

Copy holder

Neutral wrist position

Chair supports curve of back

90°

Wrist rest

Leg clearance

Keyboard 24"–27" high

90°

Footrest

BORROWED SPACE

If you can't add on and don't have an extra room, then put on your thinking cap and take another approach. Closets, stairwells, and landings may have unrecognized office potential. Unless you need complete privacy, or have so much paraphernalia that square footage is critical, there is bound to be workspace available.

Space stolen from a closet can be just enough to hold a small office. In this one stock kitchen cabinets make perfect wall storage.

This high-rise desk has divided shelves and a smart stack of drawers. There is additional storage under the table.

Here is a clever way to use the space under the stairs. The tidy hideaway holds a workstation complete with cubbies and file drawers; the tambour front slides sideways. The closed top blocks dust from the open stairs.

Concrete and structural steel lend a minimalist finish to this rebuilt landing in a fire zone. Vertical blinds shade the large window, and a glass block ceiling admits light from the floor above.

STUDIOS

IF YOU ARE AN ARTIST, you no doubt have specific requirements for your studio. You may want privacy or freedom to make a mess as you work. You'll want the light to be just so, and need room for supplies. If you have a separate studio, you're ahead of the game, but an extra room, basement, or attic may be converted. Plan ahead for special ventilation, plumbing, and electrical needs, and check your local zoning and building codes.

Top left: It is hard to recognize the original garage in this gracious studio, which has everything the artist hoped for. The all-white room is flooded with light from the skylight in the ridge of a new 18-foot roof. French doors give a great view of the terrace; stock cabinets provide lots of storage; and the floor plan is open to allow easy movement. Overhead track fixtures spotlight finished work.

Top right: In a studio, safe storage for fragile artwork is always in demand. If you have a high ceiling, an overhead loft is a good solution. In this one, dowels make simple dividers; access is by a sturdy ladder that rolls along a wooden track.

Right: This wonderful studio is private, but not isolated. The free-standing building has windows on all sides; many of them are actually large doors that open onto lawn or terrace; the red paint makes a geometric contrast. The rolling island is both supply cabinet and worktable. Track and recessed fixtures supplement the classic northern light coming through the clerestory windows.

Opposite: If you've ever longed to live in a tree house, you'll understand why this artist chose an enclosed third-floor porch for a studio. Awning windows provide ventilation and a terrific view. The exposed framing, red-painted accents, and simple furnishings make this a pleasantly rustic, no-fuss workspace.

SPACE FOR KIDS

IT IS AS IMPORTANT for a child to have a good study environment as it is for you. Be sure desks and chairs are set at an appropriate height (choose pieces that can be adjusted if you can), and be extra careful with electrical wires. And don't forget that kids love to set up their own workspaces—it makes them feel grown-up. Chances are, if they like the decor, they won't mind spending time at the desk, so let them participate.

Here is a clever way to make study look like fun. The raised captain's bed is accessible by bright scarlet ladder rungs. Drawers and shelves stow clothing and gear; the desk extension sits on additional shelves. The swivel chair looks grown-up, and can be adjusted as your child gets taller.

Artistic inspiration comes naturally in this child's studio. Freehand painting trims the inexpensive wood furniture; a ragged and rolled abstract pattern gives a soft painted finish to the walls. If you are setting up a studio for a young child, be sure to choose furnishings that can take some spills—or encourage the artist to repaint them into new embellishments.

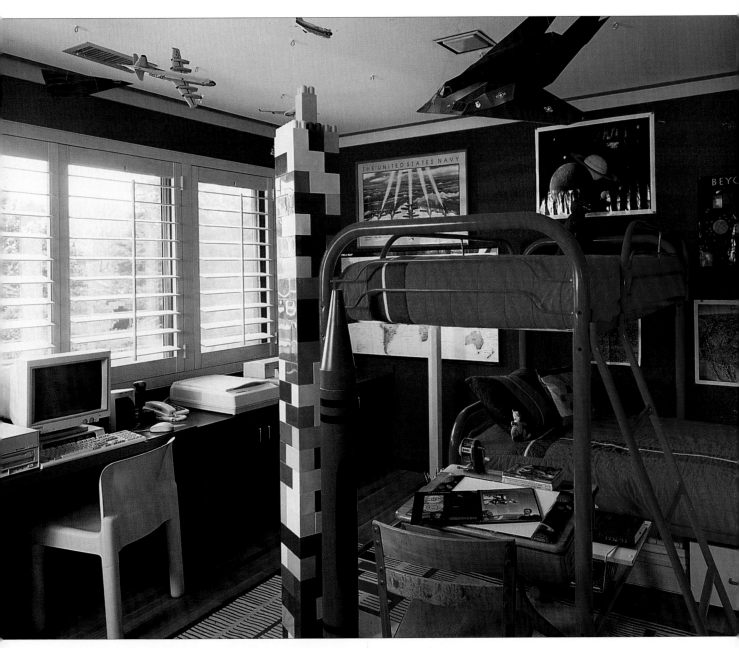

These days young scholars work with state-of-the-art equipment and may need an office setup almost as sophisticated as yours. Colorful built-ins energize this grade-schooler's domain. The laminate counter and cupboards are durable, offer maximum work surface, and have plenty of storage. The old-fashioned wood desk seems whimsical in this setting.

EXERCISE ROOMS

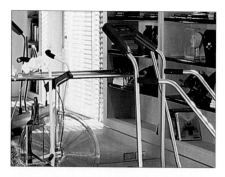

IF WORKING OUT is part of your daily routine, and you have even a little extra space, why not dedicate some of it to exercise equipment? Choose a dressing area, part of a bedroom, or fix up a basement. Many people like to put exercise rooms near the bath—or put a shower near the workout area. Choose a space that is large enough for your gear; install the proper electrical support; and put in a good media system if you like.

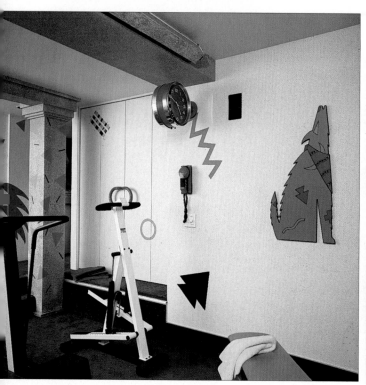

Clever use of paint transformed this basement from dark and dreary to energy central. Graphics dress up boxy structural columns; random images splash across the walls to enliven a morning workout. There is plenty of space for equipment; carpeting is soft underfoot. The red phone and industrial clock are great touches.

If you like to mix work and play, consider this dual use of space, where a great home gym meets a great home office—mixing aerobics and electronics in one room. The mirror seems to double the space, making it look less crowded than it is.

OFFICE
Questionnaire

Before you rush off to empty the linen closet or dry out the basement, work out a wish list for the kind of office you're looking for. Some of your requirements will be structural or equipment-based; others will relate more to your own personal work style. As plans take shape, test them against the questions listed below. Also refer to Planning an Office Layout on page 175, and A Look at Ergonomics on pages 178–179.

- Are there any zoning restrictions that apply? Is parking adequate?
- What about privacy? Will you be disturbed by family members? Will household noise be transmitted over the phone? Will you be able to concentrate with loud traffic or neighbors outside?
- If clients call on you, will the space project a suitable image? Is there room for a conference table and seating? When visitors approach your office, will your entire house (and family) be on display?

- Will you be working at night? With clients? Is outdoor lighting sufficient?
- Is security an issue?
- Do you need a separate outside entrance?
- How many people will work in your office? Will they need privacy? Will special soundproofing be required?
- What is the desired ambience? Corporate? Casual? Studio or atelier?
- What sort of furnishings do you want? Ready-made? Custom-made? Do you need a sofa and easy chairs as well as a desk? A conference table? A computer workstation? Rolling chairs?
- List the office equipment you use: Computer? Printer? Copier? Phone? Answering machine? Fax? VCR? TV? Cassette player? Other?
- Do you want an audio system? Video? Film? As part of your work equipment or for ambience?
- Will you have to add electrical circuits? Add or extend phone lines?
- Do you need a kitchenette? Bar? Powder room?
- What are your storage needs? Long term? Short term? Letter files? Legal files? Flat files? Bookshelves? For stationery and office supplies? For materials or samples? Will you be storing or archiving clients' materials?
- Do you need a separate area for a postal scale, copier, project bins, or sample books?
- What sort of closets do you need? Coat? Other storage?
- Do you need extra bookshelves or space to display products?
- What sort of cabinet and table

surface materials? Wood? Laminate? Stone? Solid surface? Something unique to your craft?
- What flooring do you have? Do you need new flooring? Carpeting? Wood? Vinyl? Ceramic tile? Stone? Other?
- What are present wall and ceiling coverings? What wall treatments do you like? Paint? Wallpaper? Wood? Faux finish? Plaster? Glass block?
- What sort of window treatments are required? To provide privacy? To cut glare?
- Is the lighting—both natural and artificial—sufficient? Do you need a view, or would one cause needless distraction?
- What lighting type is desired? Incandescent? Fluorescent? Halogen? What fixture types? Recessed downlights? Track lights? Pendant fixtures? Undercabinet (or shelf) strips? Indirect soffit lighting?
- Consider any other structural additions: Skylights? Greenhouse window or sunroom? Other?
- Are the area's heating, cooling, and ventilation systems adequate to handle your office needs?
- What time framework do you have for completion?
- What budget figure do you have in mind?

MAKING SPACE FOR AN OFFICE

If you can't fit your office into a closet, but don't have a self-contained room to dedicate to work, consider dividing a large room to keep work from spilling into some other part of your life. If you are worried about blocking light and air, or feeling cramped, don't despair—here is a way to have two-rooms-in-one.

If you live and work in a one-room apartment, you may find it difficult to keep business separate from pleasure. This clever room divider masks a fully furnished office without encroaching on living space.

The L-shaped divider keeps the office neatly confined; light and air passing through the partial walls preclude claustrophobia. Yet the middle band has a weighty task—as an unobtrusive extra bookshelf. A divider like this is not load-bearing, and really couldn't be simpler for a good do-it-yourselfer to adapt.

LIGHTING OPTIONS

Good workspace lighting saves eyesight and keeps spirits from flagging—your home office shouldn't feel like a dark hole—so choose fixtures that work hard. There are lots of stylish options for track, table, and pendant fixtures; be conservative or go for a conversation-maker.

Adjustable clamp-on lamps, long standard issue for drafting tables, are perfect for any desk with a lip to accept them. These, with green glass shades, seem appropriately planetary here.

Here, carefully placed fixtures balance the natural light. A stylish pendant illuminates the desk. Some of the recessed fixtures light the credenza; others, with louvers, accent the art.

A handsome chrome-finished cylindrical fluorescent fixture gives a high-tech finish to this architect's file room. Note the coiled electrical supply cord wrapping the support cable.

Bounce lighting (a photographers' trick) spreads indirect, glare-free illumination over a wide area. A white cloth draped from this ceiling reflects the beam from a halogen lamp.

You don't have to use industrial, corporate, or avant-garde fixtures in a home office; any table lamp that suits your decor is a perfectly fine choice for desktop task lighting.

Sleeping Spaces

*F*lexible, hardworking, and fun, today's bedrooms must meet our needs for efficient yet stylish private retreats. Of course we sleep in them, but we also read, lounge, exercise, work, and pamper ourselves there, away from the main bustle of the house. If you are designing

a bedroom for yourself, its ambience should reflect your taste and suit your habits. If you are setting up a guest room, it should be welcoming, but not so full of personality that it overwhelms; if it doubles as an office, plan for both uses. And your child should want to go to his room—but you should want to go there, too.

No matter the style of decor, every bedroom should have good reading light, bedside tables, carpeting or rugs, and window treatments that assure darkness and privacy. Adequate closet and bureau space is a must. A fireplace or access to a deck makes a bedroom special; incorporate them if space and budget permit.

An eclectic assortment of furnishings pulled together with panache gives this bedroom an exotic but restful ambience. The antique screen forms a translucent backdrop, and the white comforter is a great foil for the graphic upholstered bed and pillows. A good eye is essential for creating a decor like this—each piece must be special but in balance with the rest.

EN SUITE

MANY MASTER BEDROOMS are private living quarters, sanctuaries offering escape from the pressures of daily routines and space to read, relax, or sometimes to work. You may have a suite of rooms—bed, bath, dressing—or a bedroom and bathroom large enough to provide sitting and dressing areas. List the uses to which you put your master suite, and plan your decor to be practical as well as aesthetically pleasing.

Opposite: Decidedly modern, this spacious master suite's U-shaped layout includes garden access, built-in seating, and a bedroom office on the far side of the two-sided fireplace. Textured concrete, rag-painted walls and ceiling, and tightly woven wool carpet form a neutral background for the shimmering copper soffits, mirrored wall, and plaid silk bedcover. Accessories are limited, and bold.

Below: The sitting area in this large formal bedroom has a period feel in keeping with the draped four-poster bed. The symmetrical arrangement features a wonderful gathering of prints and patterns. A shared rose and ecru palette settles them successfully in quiet tête-à-tête. The sprigged carpet lightens the room, and the area rug gives focus to the design.

The sleeping area of this master suite is in full bloom. Carpet, curtains, comforter, flounce, pillows, and bed bonnet blossom—even the chair seat in the foreground has a stylized floral cover. Handpainted garlands continue the theme on walls and ceiling. Elegant furniture and a few subtle stripes keep the florals under control. Note the fabric-covered chain on the fanciful chandelier.

The adjacent dressing area is a transitional passage between bedroom and bath. The carpet flows from room to room; the striped fabric is repeated on the daybed upholstery; the same garlands dress the walls. The beautiful double vanity is topped by striking beveled mirrors and pretty sconces.

Soft colors and pretty iron furniture set the stage in this bedroom sanctuary, where bed and window curtains promise quiet seclusion. Tone-on-tone pattern gives the room a little texture—twined ribbons are painted on the walls; pieced fabrics cover the bed and window cornices; a plaid in the same tones covers the chair seat and bench. A woven rug tops the carpet.

The bed in this fresh-as-springtime master suite is in a dormer and sits right under the roof; rafters and plank ceiling are painted white. A cloud valance with poufed legs tops the window bay; the window seat is filled with pillows. Note that almost everything in this room is trimmed—contrasting piping, bindings, and ruffles abound. Even the white linens have cutwork at the hems.

The sitting area provides temporary quarters to a nursery. Once the child grows, the room will revert to adult use. In the meantime, the coordinated florals provide a picture-perfect setting for a classic iron crib and an assortment of bunnies. Note how the wall and fabric prints switch positions in the room beyond.

BEDROOM
Questionnaire

The following questionnaire will give you a starting point when designing a bedroom. Note your answer to each question on a separate sheet of paper, adding any important preferences or dislikes you may have. Then gather your notes, any clippings you've collected, and a copy of your base map (see pages 276–277 and refer to the illustration at right), and you're ready to begin your design.

- Who will use the bedroom? Yourself? Guests? Teens? Children?
- What other activities will the room accommodate? Study or office? Exercise? Hobbies?
- Do you want to include media equipment? A telephone? Does wiring need updating?
- How will you ensure privacy? From the outside? From other family members?
- Is there to be a separate dressing area? Walk-in closets? What sort of storage cupboards? Where are the mirrors?

- Do you want a sitting area? A fireplace?
- Is there an adjacent bathroom? Do you need to include a linen closet? Do you need to make plumbing alterations?
- What about furniture? What size is the bed? Is there a dresser? Side tables? Blanket chest? Coffee table? Easy chairs? Window seat? Bookshelves?
- What flooring do you have? Do you need new flooring? Wood? Vinyl? Carpeting?
- What are present wall and ceiling coverings? What wall treatments do you like? Paint? Wallpaper? Wood? Faux finish? Plaster?

- What decorating style do you want? What color scheme?
- What sort of window treatments do you want? For ambience? To provide privacy?
- Lighting type desired? Incandescent? Halogen? What fixture types? Recessed downlights? Track lights? Pendant fixtures? Floor lamps? Or table lamps?
- Consider any other structural additions? Skylights? Greenhouse window or sunroom? Other?
- What time framework do you have for completion?
- What budget figure do you have in mind?

BED CLEARANCE GUIDELINES

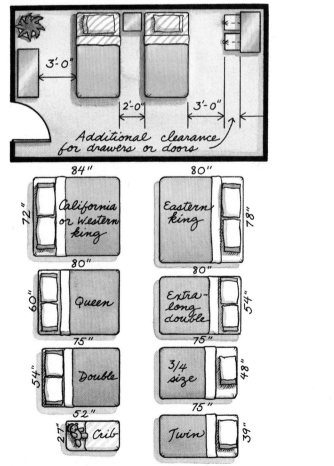

DRESSING ROOMS

Grooming is an important part of daily routine, so setting up a well-organized dressing area is a worthwhile idea. Even if you can't devote a whole room or passageway to a boudoir, there are many things you can do to enhance drawers, shelving, and closets so your wardrobe always stays under control.

Built-in closets with mirrored doors, carpeting, draperies, framed prints, and a comfortable chair make this a dressing area one could practically live in. Closely spaced shelves keep stacked garments manageable.

If you've ever planned an outfit only to find wrinkles at the last moment, you'll be glad to have a fold-up ironing center on hand.

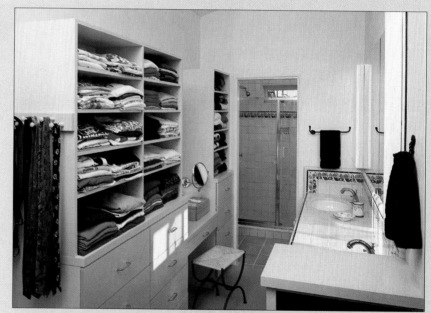

There is no wasted space in this passageway vanity-dressing area, which links bath with bedroom. Built-ins provide drawers, cubbyholes, pegs, and adjustable shelves. When not in use, the bench at the little makeup area can be pushed out of the way under the counter.

Above: Paired vanities offer storage; drawers in between double as a bench.

Far left: Custom-fitted drawers put an end to jumbled accessories. A felt pad keeps jewelry from rolling around; dividers keep ties from getting crushed, or organize socks or belts.

Near left: Special hardware makes pull-out units with a flight of shelves good for keeping things organized.

ADULT AND GUEST BEDROOMS

WHETHER YOU ARE FURNISHING A BEDROOM for yourself or guests, it should be welcoming and promise a good night's sleep. You'll want bedside tables, good reading light, window treatments for privacy, a chair, and a rug to cushion bare feet. If you are planning for guests, small touches like books, toiletries, and fresh flowers make a world of difference. You can create any ambience, or follow any style you like.

This large bedroom is furnished with traditional decorum. A formal four-poster bed rests opposite the welcoming fireplace. A pretty faux mirror is painted on the wall over the mantel, and a swag of everlastings hangs over the bed, but otherwise the accessories in this room are quite simple—just a few framed photos and some decorative pottery.

Quiet colors temper the playful spirit of this offbeat room. Sponge-painted walls are topped with a formal stenciled border; pale diamond-shaped pickling flickers over the floor. The slouchy striped curtains add to the slightly risqué ambience. This room gets a lot of character from the unusual brick fireplace and other eclectic touches.

The contemporary styling of the wrought iron bed sets the minimalist tone in this spare room. But everything one could need is nearby—good daylight, a night table on each side of the bed, and good reading light. The gray and taupe bedcover is perfect with the iron furnishings.

Not every guest room can accommodate a full-size bed, but a well outfitted single bed will be just as welcome to a solitary visitor. Here a brass bed is borrowed by furry residents, who will relinquish it when asked. Sunny striped wallpaper picks up the gold accent in the plaid that's on the bed and windows. A desk provides a spot for reading or writing.

Hideaway beds are great space-savers in small apartments or guest rooms that double as something else. In this library, painted trompe l'oeil books sit on molding-trimmed "shelves." When bedtime arrives, the wall folds forward to reveal a pull-down Murphy bed. You can face a Murphy bed to match any sort of decor—paint, paneling, wallpaper—make it look like a closet, or give it fanciful treatment such as this.

The bedding has been dressed to match the library decor, so the room looks terrific, even if the bed stays down for the duration of a visit. The same green paint lines the cabinet as backs the bookcases, and framed prints on the wall are a nice touch.

HEADBOARDS

If you want to give a unique finish to your bedroom—and transform a boring mattress and box spring on a metal frame—consider a built-in headboard. Why not design one that ties in with the style of your decor and includes lighting fixtures or handy storage cubbies?

This elaborate built-in headboard provides display space, storage, bedside tables, and lighting (fluorescent tubes in the soffit, controls on the wall) in one dramatic piece of furniture.

A tall slanted headboard provides support for pillows and makes a good backrest for reading in bed. This one, tiled with terra-cotta in the Southwestern mode, has an attached matching bedside table.

A curved, rough-combed concrete wall is an unusual choice for a headboard; this contemporary piece includes glass-block inserts lit from
behind. The crinkled silk comforter reiterates the textural effect.

KIDS' BEDROOMS

ADULTS USE MANY ROOMS of the house, but kids pack most of their living into a single room. To a child a bedroom is a place to listen to music, play games, sprawl on the floor, roughhouse, read, study, and stash innumerable possessions. That's asking a lot from four walls. Creative planning and thinking will help you to design a room that serves all those functions—and looks cool enough to please your child.

In decorating, a couple of clever accessories can really grab attention and set the tone—this is as true in the nursery as anywhere else. A grand humorous montage of baby photos will bring an instant smile to anyone who sees it, and may amuse your tyke as well. A fanciful, hand-painted changing table can be used to store and display toys later on.

KIDS' BEDROOM Questionnaire

The following questionnaire will give you a starting point when designing a child's bedroom. Remember that kids really live in their rooms, so balance your preferences with those of the child. Then gather your notes, any clippings you've collected, and a copy of your base map (see pages 276–277 and refer to the illustration on page 199), and you're ready to begin.

- How old is the child? Teenage? Grade school? Toddler? Infant?
- Is the room for one child? Two? Do you need to assure private space for each? Is it shared by a pet? Will there be room for "sleep-overs?"
- What other activities will the room accommodate? Study? Exercise? Hobbies? Music?
- Is there a play or sitting area? Any special furniture? Are there collectibles to be displayed? What sort of shelves are needed?
- Do you want to include media equipment? A telephone? Does wiring need updating?

- How will you ensure privacy? From the outside? From other family members? Is soundproofing an issue? Can you hear an infant cry from elsewhere in the house? Would you like to have an intercom?
- What sort of closets? Walk-in? Wall? What sort of storage cupboards? Where are the mirrors? Is everything at an appropriate height?
- Is there an adjacent bathroom? Do you need to make plumbing alterations? Is there secure storage to keep pharmaceuticals out of small hands?
- How many years do you expect this decor to last? Is the child old enough to take care of it? Does the child want to participate in the decorating process?
- What decorating style does the child want? What color scheme? How do you feel about these?
- What about furniture? What size is the bed? Is there a dresser? Side tables? Toy chest? Easy chairs? Window seat? Bookshelves? Is built-in furniture appropriate? Is the furniture of a scale appropriate to the child? Will it grow with the child?
- What sort of window treatments does the child want? For ambience? To provide privacy? Can the cords be stowed safely?

- What lighting type is desired? Incandescent? Halogen? What fixture types? Recessed downlights? Track lights? Pendant fixtures? Floor or table lamps? Are outlets conveniently sited to preclude extension cord use?
- Consider any other structural additions? Skylights? Greenhouse window or sunroom? Other?
- Does the room need new flooring? Wood? Vinyl? Carpeting?
- What are present wall and ceiling coverings? What wall treatments does the child like? Paint? Wallpaper? Wood? Faux finish or trompe l'oeil? Should it be scrubbable?
- Are there maintenance concerns? Should everything be easy to clean?
- Are there any special safety concerns? Is everything sturdy? Do you need window guards? Outlet covers? Do chest lids have safety hinges? Are storage hooks above or below the child's eye level? Is there a radiator that should be screened? A fireplace? Are there steps that need a gate? Do rugs have skidproof backing? If you live in an older house, has lead paint been removed?
- What time framework do you have for completion?
- What budget figure do you have in mind?

Sleigh beds are special. They have a nostalgic link to the past and seem cozy and private. This room is furnished for a young girl, but is not childish. Rather, the charming country furnishings assure that it will comfortably grow up with her. The upper walls are fabric lined, the comforter and pillows covered in a reproduction toile print.

A pretty pastel scheme can set the stage for a decor that will continue to delight as a child moves from nursery through grade school. Here a white iron bed under a border of frolicking bears is the perfect place for dreaming. Note the wonderful window treatment—painted blinds topped by striped scalloped awnings that double as swings for furry pals.

When space is at a premium, consider a loft bed for a child old enough to deal with a ladder—it will let you fit storage and sleeping quarters into a small area. Loft beds, built high up and enclosed on three sides, are also fun and seem very, very private.

This cleverly designed bed is actually half of a Victorian four-poster positioned over modular shelving. The lower bins do triple-duty as bench, storage, and step stool. Note the pillow-high sconce.

Kids love the out-of-the-ordinary when it is designed especially to suit their needs. Built on an irregularly shaped platform, this young musician's bed is close to all the action—drums, stereo system, and books. The carpeted lower step is an inviting place to lounge and visit with friends, and it also muffles some of the noise.

Here is a clever way to put an end to shared-room squabbles. A partition covered in wallpaper provides young siblings with privacy and their own territory; a personalized border placed over the beds identifies each child's domain. A consistent use of color and prints help unify the separate spaces.

CLOSET PLANNING

Both wall and walk-in closets have their advantages; with good space planning, either can hold a lot. The drawing gives measurements that will help you to plan an efficient closet system. Here are some points to consider.

- Before you purchase any storage aids or design a new closet, take careful stock of what you need to store and eliminate clothing that you don't, or won't, wear.
- Sort your clothing into categories and take some measurements. Measure garment length. Also measure the length of rod your clothing currently occupies.

Measure height, width, and depth of folded items.

- Shelves, drawers, pull-out bins, and racks can make a closet more efficient. Several manufacturers offer modular closet systems.
- Closed storage, such as bags, bins, and drawers, provides extra protection from dust, but may be hospitable to mildew.

CLOSET PLANNING AT-A-GLANCE

11"
6"
9"
38"
36"
34"
50"
65"
12"   (6 shirts)
30"
18"
17-½"
7"
12"
5"

SPACE SAVERS IN KIDS' ROOMS

Coping with skimpy space in a child's bedroom is a common problem. Here are some ways to maximize your child's territory.

- A loft bed makes optimum use of floor space because so many functions are served within the footprint of the bed. The sleeping area is on top, with a storage, play, or study area beneath.
- Stacking bunk beds take up the space of a single bed, yet accommodate two kids. If there's only one child, the extra bunk serves as both play space and guest accommodation.
- A disappearing bed, such as a wall bed, clears the decks for play or hobbies.
- Under-bed drawers, offered as accessories for many types of beds, utilize what would otherwise be wasted space. Bins, boxes, and other portable storage units that fit underneath the bed are just as useful.
- Hooks, shoe bags, and pouches hung on chair-rail molding or on the back of closet or room doors provide off-the-floor storage.
- A hinged work surface or table folds against the wall when not in use, liberating floor space for other activities.
- Shelving units that hang on the wall instead of sitting on the floor free up floor space.
- An organized closet with shelves, stacking baskets, and other modules holds much more than a standard one.
- A minimum of furniture makes the room seem more spacious. Look for multipurpose pieces, such as a toy box with a bench top or a bed with built-in storage drawers.

Neatly stored doesn't have to mean hidden from view. Pegboards and small hanging shelves, like this playfully painted one, can be part of the decor *and* the organization.

Organize your child's closet by installing a flexible storage unit. These laminate components are divided to hold pint-sized outfits.

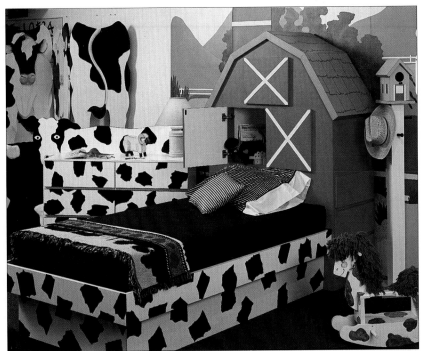

A room that has a fun decor will be a lot more fun to keep tidy. Lest one be in doubt, this youngster longs to live on a farm. A stylized landscape painted on the wall sets the scene—the headboard barn is a cupboard; the bureau masquerades as a cow; the clothes tree is topped by a birdhouse; and a trio of large cows in the background is a hinged room screen.

This one-of-a-kind bench is more than just a comfy place to lounge and read—the cutouts turn the base into a dollhouse. So next time your small fry ask for a story, suggest that they tell you one about the folk who live under the arches. As your children get older, the recesses can be used to store other decorative items, or books and magazines.

LIGHTING OPTIONS

Gone are the days when bedrooms were lit with harsh, glaring ceiling globes. Today you can design lighting that is bright or soft, where and when you want it to be. Plan for appropriate bulbs, dimmers, and multiple switch locations—then go modern or traditional, as suits your decor.

You want good but glare-free light in a walk-in closet so you can see your wardrobe. These low-voltage ring lights have a frosted glass diffuser and are a handsome fixture choice.

Avoid the jarring transition from darkened bedroom to brightly lit hallway by using track lighting with mini-reflector bulbs. This custom pewter system has lily-shaped shades accenting artwork.

If you like to read in bed, consider this: A swinging-arm fixture has been custom-fitted to a mounting block; it rides up and down the bedpost, tightening with the turn of a screw.

When it is time for relaxing here the downlights are turned off, leaving an indirect glow from strip lights hidden behind the crown moldings. Note the classic pharmacy lamps at bedside.

The soffit that extends over the bed adds intimacy to this contemporary room, and holds recessed down-lights. Bedside lighting comes from appropriately large sculpture-like lamps.

Inexpensive paper shades are a quick fix for bare bulbs or ugly fixtures. This one has been sponged with turquoise paint and then spattered with purple. Marker drawings would also be fun.

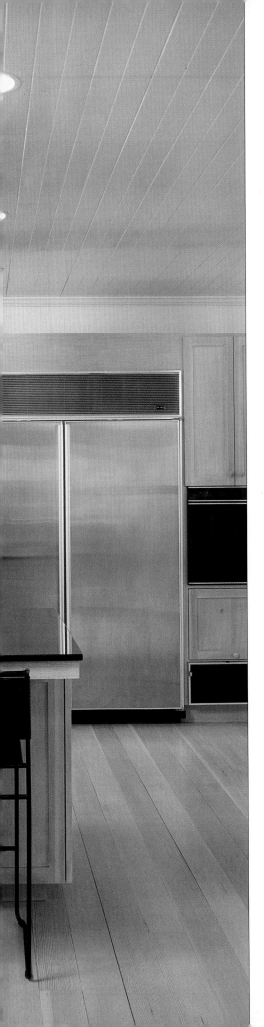

Kitchens

Perhaps the most-used and hardest-working room in a home, a kitchen should be efficient and comfortable. Style-wise, a kitchen may match or contrast with the rest of the house; design-wise, it should function as you need it to. Whether you lean toward the sleek contemporary lines of European style, a classic traditional look, the casual ambience of country, or the wittily offbeat, take time to analyze the space you'll be working with, make a list of the critical and dream features you'd like to incorporate, work out your plans on paper, and do preliminary shopping and budgeting. Expect to make adjustments to assure that space, needs, and funds are in line.

You'll find many examples of successful kitchens on the following pages. Browse through them; adapt concepts that appeal so they suit your needs; and feel free to interpret any of the ideas with fixtures, materials, and colors that suit your style.

A successful blend of traditional and modern elements creates a kitchen with timeless yet very contemporary appeal. The pale frame-and-panel cabinetry, board ceiling, wainscoting, and plank floor pay their respects to other eras. Here they combine effortlessly with shiny granite countertops, sleek stainless and black appliances, and elegant bar stools.

CONTEMPORARY KITCHENS

CUTTING EDGE KITCHENS are bright, shiny, and efficient. They are stylish rooms where cooking is serious business. Think white, think laminate, stone, stainless steel. Think high-tech fixtures and mini-blinds. Think storage—a place for everything, everything out of sight when not in use. But contemporary doesn't mean grand; in fact, a small streamlined room can be a very pleasant workspace.

Though the first thing that strikes you about this kitchen is the clean black-and-white color scheme, it has many features that make it a pleasure to cook in as well as to look at: two ovens, a warming tray, impervious counters, and lots and lots of storage. The room is flooded with light from the pop-out window.

Once a small galley, the kitchen was expanded at both ends. At the near end, an angled peninsula holds a breakfast counter and a cooktop with an arresting custom copper vent hood. The Eurostyle cabinets have raised panel doors; matching doors mask the side-by-side refrigerator.

Opposite: The unexpected soaring ceiling and sleek laminate cabinets give this kitchen a look of vast efficiency—it is not really very large, but a good floor plan makes it efficient indeed. Gleaming granite countertops, black ovens, and a dark slate floor break up the dazzling white.

IF YOU WOULD LIKE your kitchen to be a relaxing gathering place, give it plenty of seating and work space. Aim for a look that is open, uncluttered, and efficient but not slick; inviting and comfortable but not quaint. Install professional appliances if you like, but balance them with matte rather than shiny cabinets. For a timeless design, choose simple cabinetry, utilitarian work surfaces, white or natural wood, and minimal decoration.

A big island provides work space and focuses attention on the view in this formal country kitchen. Lightly pickled pine cabinets, pale countertops, creamy walls, and buff stone floor get gentle accents from the soft blue tiles and green valance; this room feels light, warm, and friendly. There is plenty of room for a crew of cooks or dawdling coffee drinkers.

Knotty pine cabinets, oak floor, and pineceiling set the tone in this large country kitchen, but there is nothing rustic or primitive about it. Bright white countertops, cobalt blue tiles, and great mustard-colored window trim are a crisp and lively foil to all the wood. Observe the smart choice of white, rather than stainless, for faucet and cooktop.

Cream-colored walls tie together the vintage white cabinets and butcher-block counters and worktable in this unpretentious kitchen. The original stove is capacious by contemporary domestic standards and looks perfectly at home under the generous new white vent hood. Simple display shelves balance the hood, adding focus without weight or clutter.

ECLECTIC KITCHENS

THOUGH KITCHENS ARE WORKPLACES filled with appliances, there is no reason to let function dictate form. If you have visions of a kitchen with a truly distinctive or offbeat character, indulge them. How to begin? Base your design on a theme rather than a specific style—perhaps a collection, motif, or color scheme. Choose assorted cupboards rather than banks of matching cabinets. Trust your eye; add things you love.

This great old-fashioned kitchen has a decidedly European air. The large undermounted sink has a varnished wood counter with a high backsplash and hot and cold taps. Sheer sash curtains are gathered top and bottom, and leave the top of the tall windows open. But it is the exuberant cabbage print that gives this room so much style—a little bit goes a long way, and it's irresistible.

KITCHEN
Questionnaire

This questionnaire provides a good starting point for discussing your ideas with architects, designers, or showroom personnel. Note your answer to each question on a separate sheet of paper, adding any important preferences or dislikes you may have. Then gather your notes, any clippings you've collected, and a copy of your base map (see pages 276–277), and you're ready to begin.

- What's your main reason for changing your kitchen?
- How many people are in your household? List adults, teens, children, pets.
- Are you right-handed? Left-handed? How tall?
- Will this be a two-cook kitchen?
- Do you entertain frequently? Formally? Informally? Do you like great-room (open-plan) designs?
- What secondary activity areas do you want? Baking center? Planning desk? Breakfast nook? Laundry and ironing center? Wet bar? Other?

- Would you like an island or a peninsula?
- Can existing plumbing be moved? To where?
- Is the kitchen located on the first or second floor? Is there a full basement, crawl space, or concrete slab below? Is there a second floor, attic, or open ceiling above?
- If necessary, can present doors and windows be moved?
- Do you want an open or vaulted ceiling?
- What's the range of your electrical service?
- What type of heating system do you have?
- Is the kitchen to be designed for a physically challenged person? Is the individual confined to a wheelchair?
- What style is your home's exterior?
- What style would you like for your kitchen? (For example, high-tech, country, contemporary, French country.) Do you favor compartmentalized European layouts or a more open, informal look?
- What color schemes do you prefer?
- List new cabinet material to be used: wood, laminate, or other? If wood, should it be painted or stained? Light or dark? If natural, do you want oak, maple, pine, cherry?
- Cabinet requirements: Appliance garage? Pull-out shelves? Lazy Susan? Tilt-down sink front? Pantry pack? Storage wall with pull-out bins? Tray divider? Spice storage? Breadbox/flatware drawer? Wall oven cabinet? Built-in microwave? Vent hood? Built-in refrigerator? Utility cabinet?

Cutting board? Knife storage? Wine rack? Wastebasket? Glass doors? Open shelving? Other?
- Should soffit space above cabinets be boxed in? Open for decorative articles? Cabinets continuous to ceiling?
- What countertop materials do you prefer: Laminate? Ceramic tile? Solid surface? Butcher block? Stone? Stainless steel? Do you want a 4-inch or full backsplash? More than one material?
- List your present appliances. What new appliances are you planning? What finish: white, black, matching panel?
- Would you prefer a vent hood or downdraft system? Do you want a decorative ceiling fan?
- What flooring do you have? Do you need new flooring? Wood? Vinyl? Ceramic tile? Stone? Other?
- What are present wall and ceiling coverings? What wall treatments do you like? Paint? Wallpaper? Wood? Faux finish? Plaster? Glass block?
- What lighting type is desired: Incandescent? Fluorescent? Halogen? 12-volt or low-voltage? What fixture types? Recessed downlights? Track lights? Pendant fixtures? Undercabinet strips? Indirect soffit lighting?
- Consider any other structural additions: Skylights? Greenhouse window or sunroom? Cooking alcove? Pass-through? Other?
- What time framework do you have for completion?
- What budget figure do you have in mind?

Right: Although this kitchen means serious business, it is also a visual feast of colors and textures. Everywhere you look there is an elegant touch—a wash of blue, a plastered niche, painted detail or cleverly adapted piece of furniture. The designers call it "French Shaker" for its mix of clean lines and Old-World charm. A close look reveals all the features of the ideal efficient kitchen.

Below right: Another view shows the concrete sink and dishwasher, installed in a cabinet to resemble an old-fashioned dry sink. The beautiful hutch sports a mix of clear and grain-painted finishes and has a handy pull-out cutting board. The accessories in this room are all part of the cooking process—orderly jars of grains, beans, and pasta; racked dishes; utensils, pots, pans, and baskets.

Opposite: Here is a quirky mix of styles that takes daring to combine: vintage range, granite counters, plain and panel cabinets, a double-pedestal island, hoop-back bar stools, witty pendant lights, sleek stainless vent hood, and country stenciling on walls and floor—all in one room? The black-and-white-on-cream color scheme integrates the disparate elements.

TILE THE BACKSPLASH

The wall behind a kitchen work area is a guaranteed target for splashes and splatters. Tile is superbly durable, easy-to-clean, and can turn this potential problem area into a decorative asset. Choose hand- or factory-produced tiles, set them squarely or diagonally, and create a graphic or representational pattern.

A stylized border adds a grace note behind a narrow counter. Have tiles custom-painted, buy a ready-made repeating pattern, or stencil one with glass and china paints.

Patterned tiles can lend a period or regional look, and there are many styles available. These were custom-made to replicate originals discovered during a kitchen renovation.

The platter of fruit protecting the wall behind this cooktop is important enough to stand without borders, and the niche below makes great use of the wonderful patterns available in Mexican tile. The effect is cheerfully rustic, the convenience thoroughly modern.

Painted sculptural border tiles add definition to this backsplash and stucco-covered vent hood. Storage and display space are provided by sturdy tiled shelves.

Plain white tiles set squarely above a stainless counter and range look classic and clean. Note that outlets and switches virtually disappear on this wall.

A custom arrangement of readily-available contrasting tile adds graphic interest to a simple white wall, neatly tying the sleek hood and cooktop together.

Cobalt blue tiles set diagonally behind the cooktop are the first things to grab your eye in this country kitchen. A black and white frieze trims the vent hood.

DRAMATIC KITCHENS

LARGE, OPEN, OR GREAT ROOM KITCHENS are great candidates for dramatic treatments. Rich colors, reflective surfaces, custom woodwork, and strong architectural lines add drama to the culinary mix. High-style kitchens such as these announce that a genius is at work, and that banquets are no problem. If you plan lots of deep color, bear in mind that it makes a room seem smaller, and pay extra attention to lighting.

Left: European detailing shines throughout this bold, black kitchen. The floor-to-ceiling aspen cabinets have a semiopaque stain sealed with a glossy polyester coating. The work area is an angular V-shape, and the mirrored back-splash and shiny cabinets reflect interesting fractured views.

Opposite, above: Planes and angles, frames and borders parade around this maple and granite kitchen. The ebony and mahogany frieze, stepped pass-through cupboards, and contrasting soffit and ceiling punctuate the room with color and movement.

Opposite, below: There are diamonds everywhere in this rich warm kitchen, dancing on the cabinets, etched into the glass doors, quilted on the backsplash—even the light fixtures are diamond-shaped. This is a serious cook's kitchen, with a professional range and adjacent electric wok, granite and maple countertops, and ample sinks and storage.

DECORATIVE STORAGE

A successful kitchen design includes plenty of storage, but that doesn't mean all accessories should be hidden behind closed doors. If you have kitchen gear or paraphernalia that is good looking, why not let it be part of the decor? Display cupboards, whether large or small, add panache to your decor.

This is a clever way to display and store a china collection. Dowels hold platters in shallow shelves; pitchers parade along the top; and glass-paneled swinging doors enclose a deeper cupboard.

Classic glass-paneled cabinet doors keep a kitchen looking light and airy. To make them a success, reserve them for matching sets or interesting collections, and put messy gear behind solid doors.

A wall cabinet with a frameless glass door is a great touch in a sleek contemporary kitchen. This one, flanked by dark woodwork, has a pale interior and a low-voltage downlight to showcase collectibles.

Rough-hewn storage shelves filling the niche-lined stucco walls of this wine cellar create an appealing and appropriately grottolike ambience. A counter fronting deeper bins offers display space.

COUNTERTOP MATERIALS

Countertops provide a durable surface in kitchens, bathrooms, and sometimes other work areas—and give you an opportunity to bring color and pattern into them. When selecting a material, consider whether it must stand up to water, knives, heat, or dirt—and balance these needs with your aesthetic wishes. Almost all countertop materials come in myriad colors or patterns, which you can often combine to create a custom design.

PLASTIC LAMINATE

ADVANTAGES: You can choose from a wide range of colors, textures, and patterns. Laminate is durable, easy to clean, water-resistant, and relatively inexpensive. With the right tools, you can install it yourself.

DISADVANTAGES: It can scratch, scorch, chip, and stain, and it's hard to repair. Conventional laminate has a dark backing that shows at its seams; newer solid-color laminates, designed to avoid this, are somewhat brittle and more expensive.

COST: Standard brands cost $1 to $3.50 a square foot; premolded, particleboard-backed tops in limited colors are $5 to $10 per running foot. Installed, a custom countertop with 2-inch lip and low backsplash costs from $40 to $90 per running foot (more for solid-color materials).

CERAMIC TILE

ADVANTAGES: It's good-looking, comes in many colors, textures, and patterns, is heatproof, scratch-resistant, and water-resistant if installed correctly. Grout is also available in numerous colors. Patient do-it-yourselfers are likely to have good results.

DISADVANTAGES: Many people find it hard to keep grout satisfactorily clean. You can buy grout sealers, but their effectiveness is disputed. The hard, irregular surface can chip china and glassware. High-gloss tiles show every smudge.

COST: Prices range from 50 cents to $50 per square foot. Choose nonporous glazed tiles, which won't soak up spills and stains. Installation costs vary depending on tile type and the size of the job (generally, the smaller the counter-top, the higher the per-foot price).

SOLID-SURFACE

ADVANTAGES: Durable, water-resistant, heat-resistant, nonporous, and easy to clean. This marble-like material can be shaped and installed with woodworking tools (but do it very carefully, or cracks can occur, particularly around cutouts). It allows for a variety of sink installations, including a counter with a sink molded in. Blemishes can be sanded out.

DISADVANTAGES: It's expensive and heavy, requiring very firm support below.

COST: For a 24-inch-deep counter with a 2-inch front lip and 4-inch backsplash, figure $100 to $150 per running foot, installed. Uninstalled it's about half that. Costs go up for wood inlays and other fancy edge details.

WOOD

ADVANTAGES: Wood is handsome, natural, easily installed, and easy on glassware and china.

DISADVANTAGES: It's harder to keep clean than nonporous materials. It can scorch and scratch, and it may blacken when near a source of moisture. You can seal it, but seal both sides or the counter may warp. It's a good idea to make an insert (or even the countertop itself) removable for easy cleaning or resurfacing. Or use a permanent protective sealer, such as polyurethane (but then you can't cut on it).

COST: Maple butcher block, which is the most popular, costs about $12 to $16 per square foot for $1\frac{1}{2}$-to $1\frac{3}{4}$-inch thickness. Installed cost is $50 and up per running foot, including miters and cutouts. It's sold in 24-, 30-, and 36-inch widths. Smaller pieces are available for inserts. Oak, sugar pine, cherry, and birch can also be used for counters.

STAINLESS STEEL

ADVANTAGES: Stainless steel is waterproof, heat-resistant, easy to clean, seamless, and durable. You can get a counter with a sink molded right in. It's a great choice for a part of the kitchen where you'll be using water a lot.

DISADVANTAGES: Don't cut on it, or you risk damaging both countertop and knife. Fabrication is expensive; you can, however, reduce the cost by using flat sheeting and a wood edge.

COST: The price of 16-gauge stainless (about $\frac{1}{16}$-inch thick) is about $5.50 per square foot, just for material. For sink cutouts, faucet holes, and bends and welds for edges and backsplashes, count on about 3 to 6 hours' fabrication time at about $45 per hour for an installed 6- to 10-foot-long counter. Custom detailing and high-chromium stainless up the price—as high as $300 to $500 per running foot.

STONE

ADVANTAGES: Granite and marble, both used for countertops, are beautiful natural materials. Their cool surface is very helpful when you're working with dough or making candy. They're heatproof, water-resistant, easy to clean, and very durable.

DISADVANTAGES: Oil, alcohol, and any acid (such as those in lemons or wine) will stain marble or damage its high-gloss finish; granite can stand up to all of these. Solid slabs are very expensive; recently, some homeowners and designers have turned to stone tiles—including slate and limestone—as attractive, less expensive alternatives.

COST: A custom-cut marble slab costs $40 to $70 per square foot, granite about $60 and up— polished and finished with a square or slightly beveled edge. Decorative edge details and the like add more. Marble counter inserts run $30 to $45 per square foot. Installation costs about $75 an hour.

GREAT ROOMS

OPEN-PLAN LIVING SPACES make the most of time spent at home—with no dividing walls conversation flows freely, tasks can be shared, no one is isolated or out of sight. These open rooms combine living, dining, and kitchen areas and need not be exceptionally large. In fact, once the partitions come down, three small spaces will feel quite grand. Because everything will be in plain view, select complementary furnishings and colors.

Left: A living room sits in one leg of this L-shaped great room, a dining area in the other, with the kitchen in between. In the kitchen area, the large cherry cabinet matches the living and dining room case pieces. The owners wanted a decor with the gracious atmosphere of New Orleans, so chose a hammered tin ceiling, arched windows, and ceiling fans. The sofa rests against a room divider of white counter-high cabinets.

Below left: Surrounding the island is a classic white kitchen; a second tier of cabinets meets the ceiling with a fancy crown molding. There are cupboards with sliding doors between brackets under the cabinets, and lights in the vent hood.

Opposite: There is no mistaking this vaulted space for anything but a great room. Massive beams and a soaring ceiling dwarf the furnishings; large floor tiles are a good counterpoint to the roof. There is little wall space for pictures or to place furniture against, so the effect is comfortable but spare.

Blue and white kitchens always seem fresh and inviting. Though tiny, this one opens to a pretty dining area and feels very comfortable. The round dining table, delicate side table, and open-backed chairs are good choices for a small room; heavier pieces would overwhelm it. Note the fresh-air feeling of the pale blue paint on the ceiling and upper walls.

Views from the island include the dining as well as living area; cooks can enjoy the fireplace and the light coming in the windows. The dining area has a deep, inviting window seat with built-in bookshelves. The cooktop in the island has downdraft ventilation, so there is no need for an overhead hood, which would spoil the open feeling in this low-ceiling room.

This once-small kitchen was transformed into a cozy great room when an exterior wall was pushed out to make room for a living-dining area with a fireplace. The rustic beams and columns link the areas and establish a Southwestern ambience. Note how the island extends between the columns, a good way to maximize space without compromising structural needs.

PLANNING A KITCHEN LAYOUT

An efficient kitchen is one in which the cook can work comfortably and move easily between appliances, counters, and storage areas. Many kitchen plans begin with a work triangle that connects refrigerator, range (or cooktop), and sink; ideally the sum of the legs of the triangle is between 12 and 23 feet. However, modern kitchens are expected to accommodate more than one cook and often incorporate more appliances (most cooktops do not fit over a separate oven) and special work areas (such as baking centers); it may be useful to plot additional triangles that link these.

Other important factors that influence kitchen layout are window arrangement and available wall space. Many people like a window over the sink, and this may give you a place to begin your plan. You should coordinate appliance positions with upper cabinet needs, and consider whether large items such as the refrigerator or wall ovens will block the view to adjacent spaces.

STANDARD KITCHEN DIMENSIONS

42" minimum clearance

26" minimum

Traffic Pattern

20" clearance for dishwasher loading

36" minimum

Breakfast table

Ceiling 96"

Soffit — Top of wall cabinet 84"

Highest shelf 72"

Bottom of wall cabinet 54"

42" eating counter

36" eating counter

Switches & outlets 44"

30" desk/table height

Countertop 36"

18" chair height

24"

30"–32" stool height

24" stool height

Six typical kitchen layouts, with work triangles shown, are given below. If your kitchen is part of an open living space or great room, you can adapt any of these. For a corridor or U-shaped layout, be sure that the refrigerator is not on the internal counter run, and design the back of the cabinets to complement the space they will face. Use the standard kitchen dimension drawings to allow proper distance between work areas and to plan vertical layouts.

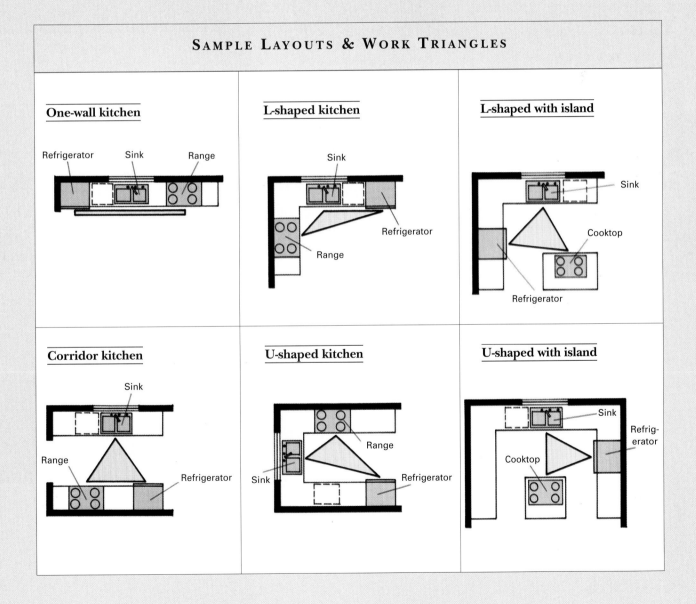

SAMPLE LAYOUTS & WORK TRIANGLES

One-wall kitchen

Refrigerator　Sink　Range

L-shaped kitchen

Sink
Refrigerator
Range

L-shaped with island

Sink
Cooktop
Refrigerator

Corridor kitchen

Sink
Range
Refrigerator

U-shaped kitchen

Range
Sink
Refrigerator

U-shaped with island

Sink
Refrigerator
Cooktop

LIGHTING OPTIONS

Plan kitchen lighting so that work areas are bright; be sure to site the lights so they won't be blocked by cooks and cast shadows. If your kitchen doubles as an eating or social center, consider controlling the ambient light with a dimmer. Then, have fun choosing fixtures.

This great-looking glass cone uses a common hundred-watt bulb to provide overhead task light for a kitchen island as well as ambient light for the room.

Incandescent mini-tubes run above these cabinets, backlighting the twig sculpture. When the house is dark, they work as nightlights, guiding the way to midnight snacks.

Undercabinet illumination provides task light and showcases accessories or an interesting back-splash. You can use incandescent or fluorescent tubes, or strip lights.

If there is no window over your sink, why not use a decorative sconce to light the washing-up? This one does double-duty as a picture light.

Tiny quartz bulbs in red pendants bring lots of light into this renovated winery. Electrical conduit, painted white, leads from roof to fixtures, which were meant to be ceiling-mounted.

Bathrooms

Cleanliness being both necessary and enjoyable, the bathroom has become a dual-purpose room where we prepare to meet the world or retreat to pamper ourselves. Bathrooms often include whirlpool tubs, fancy showers, and grooming centers; some are adjacent to exercise or dressing rooms. Many people like to have media gear and a phone available. Lighting—both ambient for mood and focused for grooming—is terribly important in a bath, as is privacy from both family and neighbors.

Most homes include more than one bathroom, and master, guest, and children's baths have different requirements that will affect the way you furnish them.

Once you analyze the way you'll use your bathroom, you can create any ambience you like, from starkly clinical to cozily old-fashioned, from sleekly modern to softly rustic, and you'll find there are fixtures and fittings to suit any style.

It is not hard to tell that these homeowners love both wood and curves. In their bath straight lines were avoided wherever possible, giving way to rounded corners, soffits, and ceiling peak. To keep the design sleek, drawers and doors were set flush, outlets and hardware concealed. That is a sauna in the center background; the toilet sits within the curved wall in the foreground.

THOROUGHLY MODERN

CLEAN LINES and sophisticated materials are the hallmarks of contemporary baths. These rooms are sleekly elegant, yet not at all clinical. They may nod to antiquity, or look toward the future, but they are designed with today's comfort and pleasure in mind—twin basins, whirlpools and showers, and superb lighting. They often include electronic gear that lets you keep up with the morning news or makes lingering a pleasure.

Imbued with serene classical elegance, this spacious room may be the ultimate two-person bath. Column-supported arches hold a pair of marble pedestal sinks, evoking the baths of antiquity in a most modern manner. The marble-tiled shower area includes two shower heads; its glass block wall diffuses light from a high window into the rest of the room.

Today, open-plan living is not limited to great rooms. This master suite features a two-sided fireplace that cheers both bed and whirlpool bath. An interesting series of steps links the two areas. The granite surround lends a formal elegance, and carpeting keeps the mood quiet. Spare furnishings and a limited palette enhance the overall serenity.

Green marble combines with light-diffusing glass blocks to give a watery ambience to this sleekly modern bath; the blocks fill a tall exterior window and divide shower and toilet areas from the vanity. Self-rimming basins are paired with Eurostyle faucets. Flush-faced laminate cabinets have simple chrome pulls. Note how the mirrored wall further reflects the shimmery light.

Attention to simple detail makes this vanity perfect for an ultramodern bath. The long glass counter has an undermounted basin, and is fronted with a stainless towel bar. At mirrorside, a diffused inset fixture provides light just where it is needed; the storage niche glows as a nightlight for the hallway beyond. This is a cleanly elegant and soothing room.

Opposite: This marble-tiled space proves that small and comfortable are not mutually exclusive terms. Toilet and vanity counter line one side of the corridor, shower and whirlpool the other. The only natural light in the room comes from a skylight, and is reflected in the large mirror. The built-in TV can be viewed from tub or shower.

BATHROOM
Questionnaire

This questionnaire provides a good starting point for discussing your ideas with architects, designers, or bathroom showroom personnel. Note your answer to each question on a separate sheet of paper, adding any important preferences or dislikes that come to mind. Then gather your notes, any clippings you've collected, and a copy of your base map (see pages 276–277), and you're ready to begin your design.

- What's your main reason for changing your bathroom?
- How many people will be using the room? List adults, children, and their ages.
- Is it a master bath? Guest bath? Kid's bath? Powder room?
- Are users left-handed? Right-handed? How tall is each one?

- How many other bathrooms do you have?
- What secondary activity area would you like to include? Garden center? Laundry facilities? Exercise facilities? Dressing or makeup area? Sauna? Spa? Audio or video system?
- Are you planning any structural changes? Room addition to existing house? Greenhouse window or sunroom? Skylight? Other?
- Is the bath located on the first or second floor? Is there a full basement, crawl space, or concrete slab beneath it? Is there a second floor, attic, or open ceiling above it?
- If necessary, can present doors and windows be moved?
- Do you want an open or vaulted ceiling?
- What's the rating of your electrical service?
- What type of heating system do you have? Does any ducting run through a bathroom wall?
- Is the bath to be used by a physically challenged person? Is the individual confined to a wheelchair?
- What style would you like for your bathroom? Do you favor compartmentalized European layouts or a more open, informal look?
- What cabinet material do you prefer: wood, laminate, or other? If wood, should it be painted or stained? Light or dark? If natural, do you want oak, maple, pine, cherry?

- What color schemes do you like?
- Storage requirements: Medicine cabinet? Linen closet? Drawers? Cabinets? Laundry hamper or chute? Rollout baskets? Open shelving? Other?
- What countertop materials do you prefer? Laminate? Ceramic tile? Solid-surface? Wood? Stone? Othe? Do you want a backsplash of the same material?
- List your present fixtures. What new fixtures are you planning? Bathtub? Shower? Tub/shower combination? Vanity? Sink? Toilet? Bidet? What finish: white, pastel, full color?
- Would you prefer natural or mechanical ventilation?
- What flooring do you have? Do you need new flooring? Wood? Vinyl? Ceramic tile? Stone? Other?
- What are present wall and ceiling coverings? What wall treatments do you like? Paint? Wallpaper? Washable vinyl wallpaper? Wood? Faux finish? Ceramic tile? Other?
- Consider natural light sources: Skylight? Window? Clerestory?
- Artificial lighting desired: Incandescent? Fluorescent? Halogen? What fixture types? Recessed downlights? Track lights? Wall-mounted fixtures? Ceiling-mounted fixtures? Indirect soffit lighting? Fan-and-light combination?
- What time framework do you have for completion?
- What budget figure do you have in mind?

TRADITIONAL CHARM

IF YOUR TASTE leans toward the old-fashioned comfort of a claw-footed tub and porcelain-handled fittings—indulge it. There is no reason not to mix nostalgic charm with contemporary convenience. Many reproduction fixtures, fittings, and tile patterns are available; marble is almost always appropriate—and attractive. Paneling, shutters, or lace at the windows, and traditional lighting fixtures are important finishing touches.

Modern convenience and traditional styling can coexist very happily. Witness this bath, which gives every indication of surviving from a bygone era, yet holds the latest fixtures. Victorian trimmings blend with a contemporary whirlpool tub; the wallpaper and tile wainscoting are timeless. The reflection shows shower alcove and a tiled privacy wall masking the toilet.

This brand-new cream and white bathroom has reproduction fixtures and fittings that give it a timeless charm. The frieze at the top of the walls is textured; it is a reissue of a traditional nineteenth-century wallcovering material. Pedestal sinks are graceful alternatives to vanity cabinets. Though they don't provide storage, they do make a room seem larger.

While a dormer almost always provides a certain nostalgic charm, it inevitably presents some logistical challenges—met here by centering the tub on the tallest part of the wall and putting the toilet out of sight under the sloping eaves. The stepped glass block walls give a feeling of privacy. Beautiful woodworking around the tub enhances the traditional mood.

Tucked behind the wall at the end of the vanity—and under the sloping roof—is a very contemporary shower enclosure that gets daylight from the opposite windows. It is tiled with the same rosy marble used elsewhere in the room, and has a bench with a slab top.

Opposite: This bathroom is tucked into a large dormer, which immediately gives it an old-fashioned flavor. Raised panel cabinetry and rosy marble lend an appropriate ambience while offering up-to-the-minute luxury. The mirrored wall reflects the light from a row of pretty sash windows over the tub. The traditional recessed medicine cabinet is on the side wall.

PLANNING A BATHROOM LAYOUT

The bathroom is one of the most frequently used rooms in the house, so it should be functional and durable as well as pleasant. Although governed by the space available, layout possibilities are virtually endless; you need a minimum of 5 by 7 feet for tub, toilet, and sink. When planning, list the features you wish to include (two sinks? vanity cabinet or pedestal sink? a makeup center? a separate shower?) and decide if you prefer an open or compartmentalized layout.

Be sure to consider window arrangement, privacy issues, and door swing—if space is limited, pocket doors may be ideal. If you are remodeling or renovating, existing plumbing lines may limit your choices; structural limitations may affect your choice of heavy fixtures such as a whirlpool bath, or dictate flooring. Tubs, showers, and sinks come in a variety of sizes and shapes, so consult a plumber or showroom about options.

STANDARD HEIGHTS

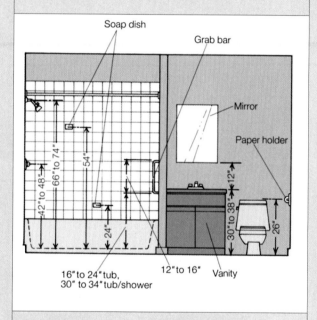

16" to 24" tub,
30" to 34" tub/shower

12" to 16"   Vanity

BARRIER-FREE GUIDELINES

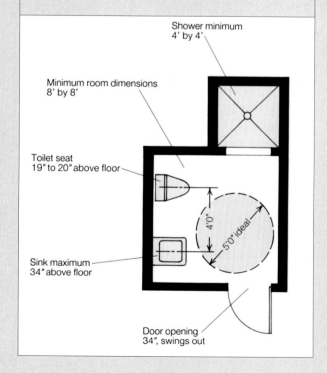

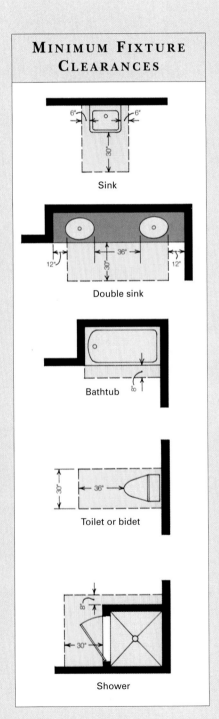

MINIMUM FIXTURE CLEARANCES

Sink

Double sink

Bathtub

Toilet or bidet

Shower

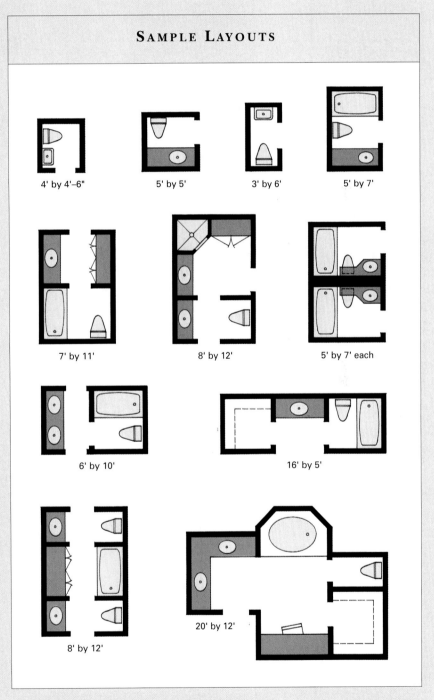

SAMPLE LAYOUTS

4' by 4'-6"

5' by 5'

3' by 6'

5' by 7'

7' by 11'

8' by 12'

5' by 7' each

6' by 10'

16' by 5'

8' by 12'

20' by 12'

The bathroom layouts above represent just a few typical configurations; the larger your room, the more design flexibility you have. Refer to the height and clearance drawings along with these layouts to start your plan.

TUBS AND SPAS

There is nothing like a long soak in a comfortable tub for soothing body and soul. Options include conventional or soaking tubs (still water) or whirlpool tubs (with circulating water) and even saunas or steam rooms. Whatever you choose, make the environment as relaxing as the fixture.

The delightful alcove containing this bath only looks like a bay window. The outer wall has frosted-glass casement windows. The return walls on each end feature etched mirror panels set into mock window sash.

This luxurious spa is set in a glass room that gives bathers the sun-and-sky view of an outdoor pool within the protection of a controlled environment. The glass block wall at the gable end allows diffused light to enter but protects users from the eyes of neighbors dwelling opposite.

Above left: There is no denying the romance of an old-fashioned freestanding tub—or the ample depth. This one is truly old, but the fittings have been reconditioned. It looks perfectly at home in a new bathroom.

Above right: The green marble deck of this second-floor bathroom bay seems to carry bathers right out into the treetops. The deep deck gives ample room for plants; leaded windows focus the view.

Above left: A deep Japanese soaking tub promises relaxation. This one catches the breezes from the windows just above. The completely tiled floor eliminates the need to have a lip on the shower alcove.

Above right: This compact, cedar-lined indoor sauna has benches for several occupants. All you need for a sauna, besides a heater, are an airtight shower door, a comfortable bench, and effective ventilation.

Fresh and Simple

IF YOU ARE DRAWN to natural materials and handcrafted detail, use them to create a bath with the freshness of a mountain spring and the convenience of hot water on demand. The keys to success? Simple details, honestly selected and sparingly used. Acknowledge the organic qualities of wood, terra-cotta, or stone by finishing them simply. Choose accessories with similar qualities; mix all with daylight, and you should be delighted.

Opposite below: This single-room suite makes the most of available space and natural light. A pillar-framed knee-wall divides the room while offering a view through French doors on the opposite wall. Rustic tiles surrounding the fixtures lend a handmade touch refined by geometric mosaic borders.

Below: An expanse of mirror makes the most of the treed landscape outside this narrow wood-lined bath, which seems effortlessly connected to the outdoors. The carefully crafted furnishings are simple and utilitarian, yet sophisticated; the vanity top is hand-tooled marble.

FINISHING TOUCHES

Attention paid to details leads to rooms that escape the ordinary. Give thought to touches that will make your bath unique and especially inviting—even if your budget is modest. Dream away…perhaps a greenhouse window, or luxurious fittings, or an extravagant basin?

A wood counter and basin are the perfect finish for a wood-lined bathroom. These were laminated from clear redwood, then carefully sealed. The brass faucet adds a warm and graceful accent.

If wall space is limited in your bath, run a towel bar along the face of the vanity. This brass bar is part of a study in matte and shiny, smooth and rough.

Why not place your vanity right in a small pop-out window? You couldn't ask for a brighter, sunnier space. Many can do double-duty as a greenhouse—just add shelves or hooks for hanging plants.

If you are artistically inclined, finish your bath with an extravagant wallpainting. This one is painted on canvas strips and has an open background for easier joining.

A great luxury, heated towel bars keep bath linens toasty and serve as radiators. This one harnesses old-fashioned hydronic power; electric versions are also available.

A massive walnut slab makes a handsome deck for a sleek, self-rimming brass basin. This one has a matching backsplash. The faucet has digital temperature controls.

This wall-mounted heated towel bar snakes back and forth for maximum warming effect. A heat lamp helps cut the chill when you leave bath or shower.

DECORATED IN STYLE

WHAT MAKES A STYLISH DESIGN? Often a specific theme lends harmony, or a visual anchor, to a room's decor. It may be a color scheme, a collection that provides a repeating motif, or an unusual attention to architectural trim. Bathrooms are as worthy of special design as any other room; in fact, they invite it. If one of these appeals, think of basing yours upon a theme with personal significance.

Opposite: A design based on a regional style is immediately distinct and cohesive. This master bath is part of an overall Oriental house design. It derives its personality from the mix of characteristic prints that cover the walls, the black lacquer trim, and the shoji screens that slide between rooms and trim the closet doors. A pierced overhead screen frames the raised bath area, which includes a deep, Japanese-style soaking tub. The shoji screen slides to reveal a conventional window.

Below: The palette is black, sand, and taupe, with amber wood accents. Stark color fields isolating particular features balance the figured papers to create a serene space. The wide lintels over the doorways extend the theme. The countertop towel stand is a perfect accessory.

Pink and white, floral and perfect. No detail escaped attention when this bathroom was designed. Every element, from the expanse of wallpaper and wainscoting to the nearly hidden tile border between windows and tub, was considered and planned—every potential problem worked out in advance. The result is charming, luxurious, timeless, and totally up-to-date.

The freestanding walk-in shower is the centerpiece of the room. It faces the tub and windows; to each side is a vanity, one of which leads to a dressing area. The gabled roof over the tub provides the space for the pediment over the shower; the pilasters continue the classical theme. Note that the floor is tiled between tub and shower only; the rest of the room is carpeted.

In this tailored bath an extra-long whirlpool tub sits in an alcove under a large, divided-light window. The arched top of the storage niche repeats the shape of the cabinet fronts and mirrors. Other fine touches include the carnelian tile dado running around the room, the complementary border inserted in the floor, and the custom wall sconces.

The green and amber room has everything that the homeowners asked for: elegance, a rich sense of color, and a touch of drama—all without being too dark. The two vanities are made of bird's-eye maple, which brings a touch of amber into the expanse of deep green. Ceiling soffits, lit by strip lights, enhance the space; the walls and ceiling were sponged and streaked.

Showers can be private and secluded, or glass-enclosed —or entire tile-lined rooms with a drain in the floor. Design yours to be as luxurious as you like. Include a high-powered water source; multiple, hand-held, or adjustable heads; a bench; a toiletry niche; even windows or a skylight.

An etched-glass shower enclosure adds a decorative accent and provides a sense of privacy. This one has Art Deco motifs and reaches from floor to ceiling.

The owners of this home wanted to recreate the experience of an outdoor shower. Boulders were hauled to the site and the room was built around them.

This walk-in shower incorporates a bench, an adjustable hand-held shower head, and a vertical grab bar, as well as towel bars and convenient toiletry niches.

This shower room features a high-power dome head; a column-mounted hand shower gives targeted washing. An overhead vent fan keeps things aired out.

An exterior shower wrapped by a curved glass wall provides a spectacular view. This one has glass blocks below for privacy. Consider omitting the roof where the climate permits outdoor bathing.

A two-person steam shower soothes muscles after a workout. This one has a built-in bench and a toiletry niche. A glass enclosure minimizes shower bulk in a small room—and doesn't block the light.

LIGHTING OPTIONS

Bathroom lighting must establish the desired ambience and provide task light that is at once gently flattering and strong enough for grooming—often in a room where mirrors and glazed tile cause unwanted glare. But you have lots of options for bulbs and fixtures; here are just a few.

Inconspicuous flush-mounted incandescent bulbs are set at intervals on this long mirrored cabinet, providing good grooming light without interrupting the reflected view.

Why not use lighting to emphasize a special detail? Here, tiny hidden strip lights accent a diamond-patterned marble border—a fun touch as a night-light or to greet guests.

To avoid heavy shadows, it is best to place mirror lights at the side, rather than directly overhead. This row of bulbs alongside a makeup mirror is a classic, evoking backstage ambience.

The scalloped soffit over this mirror is unique and sheds a warm, flattering light through its diffusing glass. For fill, fiberoptic tubes run down both sides of the maple cabinet.

As an attractive, unobtrusive option to a conventional fixture, the entire ceiling of this shower glows. The translucent glass roof is illuminated by two strong quartz spotlights hidden above.

PART 4

Planning Primer

GETTING STARTED

"**MEASURE TWICE, CUT ONCE.**" Anyone about to decorate, renovate, or build should give this carpenters' credo a broad interpretation—"Plan ahead." Before you actually begin a project, whether large or small, you should be sure you understand what is involved, and know how it will be accomplished. You'll probably start with a dream that seems perfectly clear—say, a freshly decorated living room—but you'll quickly realize that many questions must be answered before you begin. You'll see too that the answer to one question may affect the answer to another, so take your time and think things through.

DEFINING YOUR GOALS

What is the desired result of your decorating project? The answer may seem so obvious—you want the room to look wonderful and work well—but the question is not as simple as it seems.

- Why are you undertaking this project? Is it because you don't like the way the room looks, or because it no longer works well, or both? Has there been a change in your life circumstances that affects the way you use your home? Marriage, children, an empty nest, a parent coming to live with you, a change in your health, the need or desire to work from your home?
- Does the room need a cosmetic update, or a complete redo? If cosmetic, how extensive? Do you simply hate the wall covering, or do you want to replace all your furnishings? Can you work within existing walls, or do you need to make structural changes? Will you need building permits or a zoning variance?
- How is your future tied to this house? Do you plan to live there a long time? Is the house an investment? What are the economic ramifications of your decorating or home improvement project? Will this project increase the value of the house, or price it out of its neighborhood? Will you be able to get the investment back should you decide to sell? Are you trying to fix up the home so that you can sell it in the near future? If this is not your long-term home, you may want to consider how other people will feel about the aesthetic choices you make—the bright carpeting you love may strike a potential buyer as prohibitively expensive to replace.

MAKING A GAME PLAN

In decorating, the "how" goes hand-in-hand with the "why" and "what." You'll want to be sure you are able to follow through with your goals so those dreams turn into reality.

- Can you do the designing or planning yourself, or will you need or want outside help? Do you envision wanting materials or furnishings that are only available through designers or contractors?
- Will you be doing the work yourself? Do you really have the necessary skills? The tools? The time? If the job is extensive, are you prepared to coordinate subcontractors for the parts you cannot do?
- Where will you live while the work is under way? Are you prepared to live with the mess or inconvenience? These questions are particularly important if you are remodeling a kitchen or bathroom, and the answers will affect your costs—if you are moving into a rental or eating out for weeks on end, calculate these expenses.

MAKING A BUDGET

"How much will it cost?" may be your first question, but "How much do you want to spend?" is just as important. To make a budget, list all the materials you'll need, the services (labor) you'll be using, and any permits required. Then list the cost of each item, including any shipping charges or taxes. Add these figures to find the total cost; to be safe, add 15 to 20 percent as a contingency figure.

Making a budget is not a one-step process. You can't begin with-

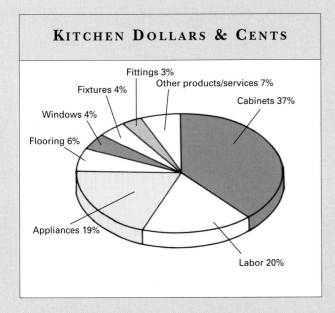

KITCHEN DOLLARS & CENTS

Fittings 3%
Fixtures 4%
Windows 4%
Flooring 6%
Other products/services 7%
Cabinets 37%
Appliances 19%
Labor 20%

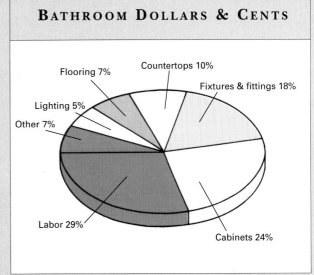

BATHROOM DOLLARS & CENTS

Flooring 7%
Countertops 10%
Lighting 5%
Fixtures & fittings 18%
Other 7%
Labor 29%
Cabinets 24%

out having some idea of your goals and game plan, because you can't list the cost for items you don't know about. At the same time, you can't have a final plan until you know if it is within your budget. Follow the steps below to calculate the potential cost of your project, then evaluate and revise your choices as necessary.

- To begin your budget, you'll have to learn the prices of potential materials. So go shopping. Visit showrooms, home centers, the lumberyard, or whichever vendor is appropriate. Get catalogs—many appliance and cabinet manufacturers have 800 numbers, and showrooms will often photocopy information for you.

- Include the small details such as hardware and bathroom fixture controls, which can be costly and add up when used in multiples.
- Include the hidden components —nails, glue, electrical wire.
- Do your math—calculate how much of everything you'll need.
- Talk to professionals to get a general idea of costs for the job you have in mind. They won't be able to give you a firm bid until you have your plans in hand, but they can advise you of usual costs.

Because of the mechanics, fixtures, and appliances involved, kitchens and baths are usually the most expensive rooms to renovate. The illustrations above show the

typical allocation of funds for remodeling either space. Bear in mind that, whatever the room, structural changes have a significant impact on the total budget for the project.

Consider also that you often get what you pay for, and invest in the best quality that you can afford—particularly if it is something that is not easy to change later.

You will probably revise your goals and plans several times before you arrive at a workable budget. The more informed you are about the available options, the more easily you will be able to select the ones that are right for you—in terms of both their cost and quality.

LIGHTING BASICS

IF UNDERSTANDING LIGHTING seems daunting, it may help to consider it from two angles. First, lighting is functional; it illuminates your living space and makes it safe and easy to do whatever you need to do. Second, lighting is aesthetic, affecting ambience by its intensity and color—and fixture style. Here are some tips to help you plan lighting and select fixtures and bulbs.

TYPES OF LIGHT

Interior lighting is referred to as being either ambient (general) or task (specific); it should come from three different sources.

NATURAL LIGHT: Daylight enters through windows, doors, and skylights. Depending upon the orientation of these, and the time of day, the season, and the weather, natural light can have a gentle or harsh effect. Natural light is primarily ambient, though it can be sufficient for daytime tasks near a window.

ARTIFICIAL AMBIENT LIGHT: Creating soft ambient lighting requires careful planning and positioning of fixtures (usually overhead). Try to avoid high contrasts from one area to another. Using several light sources (fixtures) is preferable to just one. Dimmer switches provide control and flexibility.

ARTIFICIAL TASK AND ACCENT LIGHT: Whether emitted from individual pendant, floor, or table lamps, or from track lights or undercabinet strip lights, task lighting focuses illumination on areas where vision will be concentrated—on work areas, at bedside, in reading areas. Use smaller accent lights to illuminate book or display shelves, or artwork.

PLANNING FOR LIGHTING

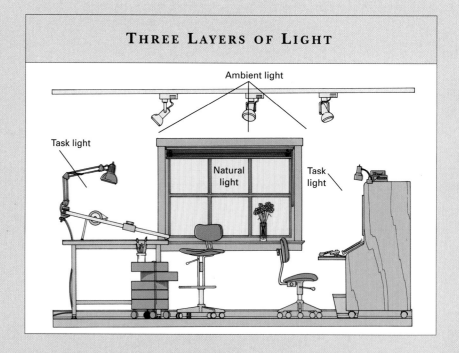

THREE LAYERS OF LIGHT

Ambient light

Task light

Natural light

Task light

In the drawing of the bedroom, opposite, natural light enters through the window; ambient light comes from recessed fixtures (A); task light is supplied by adjustable sconces (B); and artwork is accented by small track lights (C).

LIGHTING TIPS

• The style of the lighting fixtures affects ambience as well as determining the amount of illumination they provide. Consider the period and style of your decor when selecting fixtures, as you would for any accessories.

• If you opt for an eye-catching fixture such as a large chandelier or unusual pendant, don't add competing focal points.

• Many decorative fixtures are glare producers if turned on high; they don't need to carry the lighting load if other ambient and task light levels are appropriately set.

• To make a small room look larger, try uplighting a pale ceiling.

• To make a large room feel more intimate, try using spare downlighting, high-contrast or pinpoint accent schemes, or low, diffused wall sconces.

• Adequate ambient light is the key to creating a comfortable living space. Indirect cove and soffit lighting or wall washer fixtures are good choices.

• Plan lighting controls to be accessible as you move about the house. It may be convenient to have fixtures switch from more than one location.

• Light-colored countertops, work surfaces, and walls add brightness because they reflect light.

• Light at a mirror should shine on the person, not the glass.

Comparing Light Bulbs & Tubes

INCANDESCENT
A-bulb

DESCRIPTION: Familiar pear shape; frosted or clear.
USES: Everyday household use.

T—Tubular

DESCRIPTION: Tube-shaped, from 5" long; frosted or clear.
USES: Appliances, cabinets, decorative fixtures.

R—Reflector

DESCRIPTION: White or silvered coating directs light out end of funnel-shaped bulb.
USES: In directional fixtures; focuses light where needed.

PAR—Parabolic aluminized reflector

DESCRIPTION: Similar to auto headlamp; special shape and coating project light and control beam.
USES: In recessed downlights and track fixtures.

Silvered bowl

DESCRIPTION: A-bulb, with silvered cap to cut glare and produce indirect light.
USES: In track fixtures and pendants.

Low-voltage strip lights

DESCRIPTION: Like Christmas lights; in strips or tracks, or encased in flexible, waterproof plastic.
USES: Task lighting and decoration.

FLUORESCENT
Tube

DESCRIPTION: Tube-shaped, 5" to 96" long. Needs special fixture and ballast.
USES: Shadowless work light; also indirect lighting.

PL—Compact tube

DESCRIPTION: U-shaped with base; $5\frac{1}{4}$" to $7\frac{1}{2}$" long.
USES: In recessed downlights; some PL tubes include ballasts to replace A-bulbs.

QUARTZ HALOGEN
High-intensity

DESCRIPTION: Small, clear bulb with consistently high light output; used in halogen fixtures.
USES: In specialized task lamps, torchères, and pendants.

Low-voltage MR-16 (mini-reflector)

DESCRIPTION: Tiny (2" diameter) projector bulb; gives small circle of light from a distance.
USES: In low-voltage track fixtures, mono-spots, and recessed downlights.

Low-voltage PAR

DESCRIPTION: Similar to auto headlight; tiny filament, shape, and coating to give precise direction.
USES: To project a small spot of light a long distance.

PUT IT ON PAPER

DRAWINGS OF YOUR DECORATING PLANS will help you to organize your thoughts and communicate with others. You don't need to be able to make beautiful renderings, just clear sketches, drawn to scale. An accurate base map shows the floor plan; an elevation shows the arrangement of vertical features such as windows, cabinets, or bookshelves.

MEASURE THE SPACE

First, sketch out your present layout (don't worry about scale), doodling in the windows, doors, closets, and other features. Then using a folding wooden rule or a steel tape, measure each wall, plus the sizes and locations of any openings or irregularities; record the dimensions.

- Beginning at one corner of the room, measure the distance to the outside of the window frame, from there to the opposite edge of the window frame, from this edge to a built-in cabinet, and so on to the opposite corner. After you finish one wall, total the figure; then take an overall measurement from corner to corner. The two figures should be the same.
- Measure the height of the wall in the same manner.
- Do the opposite walls agree? If not, something's out of whack; find out what it is. Also check all corners with a carpenter's square or by the 3-4-5 method: measure 3 feet out from the corner in one direction, and 4 feet out in the other direction, then connect the points with a straightedge. If the distance is 5 feet, the corner is square.

MAKE A BASE MAP

Now draw your room to scale on graph paper. Most designers use ½-inch scale (1/24 actual size). An architect's scale is helpful though not essential, but using a T-square and triangle and some good drafting paper with a ¼-inch grid will make the job a lot easier.

- If you own a personal computer, you may wish to try one of the many design programs currently available. The latest offerings are considerably more user-friendly and much less costly than earlier CAD programs, which were aimed at professionals.
- The sample plans shown include dimension lines and electrical symbols—outlets, switches, and fixtures. Be sure to indicate door swings, windows, skylights, and any heating ducts or returns. If you can, it's also helpful to note the direction of joists, mark any bearing walls, and sketch in other features that might affect your remodeling plans. And if you're considering "borrowing" space from an adjacent room or hallway, be sure to add its features to your map as well.

MAKE AN ELEVATION

Elevations are particularly important when planning cabinets or wall systems.

- Try an elevation sketch of your proposed wall arrangement. How do the vertical lines created by cabinets, windows, doors, and appliances fit together? It is not necessary for them to align perfectly, but you should consider adjusting the width of a wall cabinet to line it up with the edge of a sink, range, or base cabinet.
- Follow a similar process to smooth out horizontal lines. Does the top of the window match the top of the wall cabinets? You might want to adjust the cabinet height, or add trim or a soffit.

RECORD YOUR THOUGHTS

A wish list can help organize your responses to your present room. Refer to the pertinent questionnaire (in the preceding chapters) and, over the course of a week, jot down your thoughts and impressions. Don't worry about consistency, and don't worry about cost at this point; you can always cut back later if you must.

- What do you like about your present space? What do you dislike? Do you want more morning light? Is storage lacking? To help stimulate your responses, look through the pictures here and browse through some design magazines.
- Sum up your concerns on a separate sheet of paper, adding any important preferences or dislikes that you discover. Then gather up your list, any clippings or catalogs you've collected, and a copy of your base map, and get ready to start brainstorming.

A TYPICAL BASE MAP

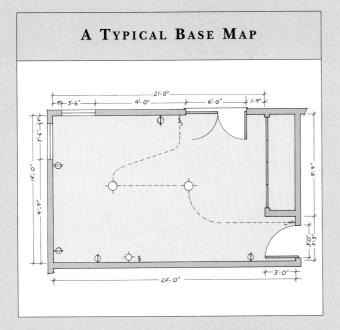

A TYPICAL ELEVATION

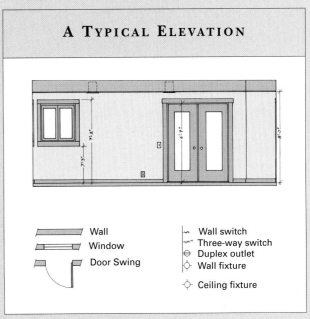

Wall	Wall switch
Window	Three-way switch
Door Swing	Duplex outlet
	Wall fixture
	Ceiling fixture

A KITCHEN BASE MAP

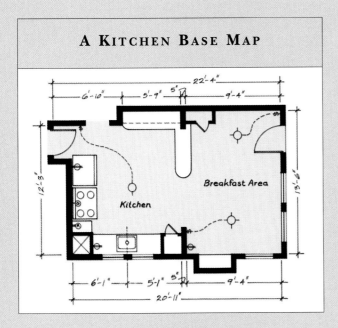

A KITCHEN ELEVATION

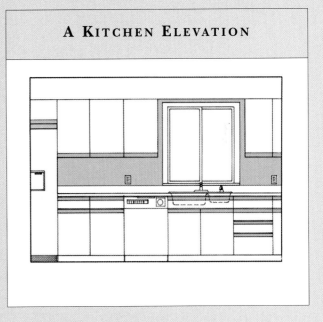

REMODELING OPTIONS

WHEN PLANNING TO REDECORATE or remodel, most of us are limited by space and layout restrictions where we currently live. Even so, you may have more choices than you think. A simple face-lift can work amazing changes. A new window bay, a walk-in closet, or a raised ceiling can make a surprisingly dramatic difference. Or maybe an attic or basement conversion can provide the quiet spot you've been looking for.

UPDATING EXISTING SPACE

One of the easiest and most instantly gratifying improvements you can make is updating. Though it won't solve underlying problems with the basic floor plan or boost available space, this type of remodel is the easiest for a do-it-yourselfer and will often do as much for a dreary room as rearranging the walls—at a fraction of the cost.

• Consider replacing old wallpaper, adding recessed downlights, rolling out a cushy carpet—you might even add new windows—to give a worn or tired room a bright, fresh look.

REDEFINING SPACE

In contrast to a simple update, reassigning interior space allows you to alter your home's floor plan to make the space you already have more usable and efficient.

• Taking down a wall or opening up a ceiling can bring in light and contribute a new feeling of spaciousness. Be careful though; removing a wall may be structurally problematic.

• Adding a wall to divide a large space can give you two separate rooms (for instance, a sleeping area and a study) instead of one. Individual spaces for sleeping and desk work needn't be huge; perhaps two people can share an existing closet area or bath. Adding a wall is usually a simple proposition.

• Another way to stretch space is to push out by adding a bay window or dormer. Such a unit can be installed where no opening existed before or replace an existing window. A cantilevered pop-out can provide several feet of new floor space—without the expense of a new foundation.

ROOM CONVERSIONS

If an interior redesign won't solve your problem, try looking up, down, and around. It's possible that at least some of the space you need already exists and can be converted to a new use. The three most obvious choices are the attic, basement, and garage. Check your local building codes first, as some restrict conversions.

• An attic room should allow a minimum of 7½ feet ceiling height over at least half of the floor area. One feature often considered a liability—the sloping walls—can become an asset with creative planning. Insulation and ventilation can help tame summer heat; dormer and roof windows help spread natural light.

• Hillside homes sometimes have substantial crawl spaces beneath the floor, perhaps reaching minimum ceiling height as the grade falls away. You may even be able to excavate and create a terrace along part of your foundation. Basement rooms can be "clammy," it's true, but with good insulation and a garden exposure you may be able to make the space quite snug and dry.

• A garage may present a great opportunity, provided you can solve the logistics of routing utilities to this location. But remember, if you cut into your garage space, you may be required to find off-street parking somewhere else.

ADDING ON

The ideal way to give yourself a substantial amount of new space is to add on. This is, of course, the most costly option, but the results may be the most satisfactory. Since blending an addition with an existing house presents both structural and aesthetic challenges, you will probably need the help of an architect or engineer. Depending upon your local building codes, you may need various permits and/or zoning variances.

- Adding laterally may be the best way to expand your house when you have a generous lot. Plan the blending of old and new spaces carefully: Be sure movement between rooms will be smooth. Consider the effect altered window arrangements will have on existing rooms. Make sure your yard or garden will still be pleasant—and can survive intrusive construction equipment.

- Adding a second floor is probably the most challenging way to remodel your house. Compared to reshaping existing space or expanding laterally, adding a second story can be demanding, expensive, and intrusive. But if your house already fills your lot, if you want to preserve garden space, or if you yearn for views beyond the neighbors' rooftops, adding a second story may be worth the trouble.

SIX REMODELING STRATEGIES

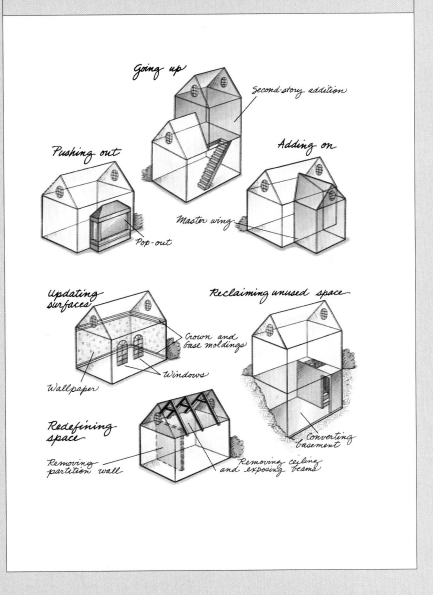

Going up
Second-story addition

Pushing out
Adding on

Master wing

Pop-out

Updating surfaces
Reclaiming unused space

Crown and base moldings

Windows

Wallpaper

Redefining space
Converting basement

Removing partition wall
Removing ceiling and exposing beams

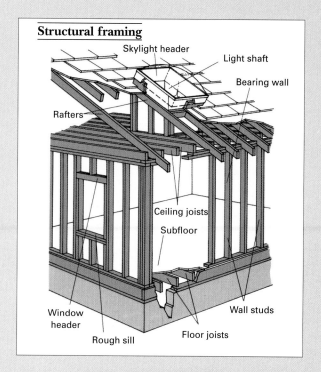

Structural framing

Skylight header · Light shaft · Bearing wall · Rafters · Ceiling joists · Subfloor · Window header · Rough sill · Floor joists · Wall studs

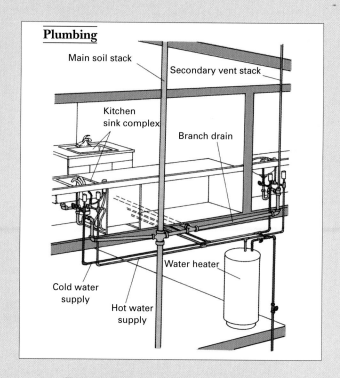

Plumbing

Main soil stack · Secondary vent stack · Kitchen sink complex · Branch drain · Cold water supply · Hot water supply · Water heater

STRUCTURAL CHANGES

Are you planning to open up space, add a skylight, or lay a heavy stone floor? If so, your remodeling project may require some structural alterations.

- As shown above, walls may be either bearing (supporting the weight of ceiling joists and/or second-story walls) or nonbearing. If you're removing all or part of a bearing wall, you must "bridge" the spot with a sturdy beam and posts. Nonbearing (also called partition) walls can usually be removed without too much trouble—unless there are pipes or wires routed through the area.
- Doors and windows require special framing as shown—the size of the header depends on the width of the opening and your local building codes. Skylights require similar cuts through ceiling joists and/or rafters.
- Planning a vaulted or cathedral ceiling instead of ceiling covering and joists? You'll probably need a few beams to maintain structural integrity.
- Hardwood, ceramic tile, or stone floors require a very stiff underlayment. Solution? Beef up the floor joists and/or add additional plywood or particle-board subflooring on top.

PLUMBING RESTRICTIONS

Suppose you wish to move a sink or tub to the other side of the room, add a kitchen island with a vegetable sink, or install a wet bar in your living room?

- Generally, it's an easy job—at least conceptually—to extend existing hot and cold water supply pipes to a new sink or appliance. The exception? When you're working on a concrete slab foundation. In this case, you'll need to drill through the slab or bring the pipes through the wall from another point above floor level.
- Every house has a main soil stack. Below the level of the fixtures, it's your home's primary drainpipe; at its upper end, which protrudes through the roof, the stack becomes a vent. A proposed fixture located within a few feet of the main stack usually can be drained and vented directly by the stack. In some areas a new island sink can be wet-vented (using an oversize branch drain as both drain and vent), but this is illegal in other areas. Sometimes a fixture located far from the main stack will require its own branch drain and a secondary vent stack of its own rising to the roof. The moral? Be sure to check your local plumbing codes for exact requirements.

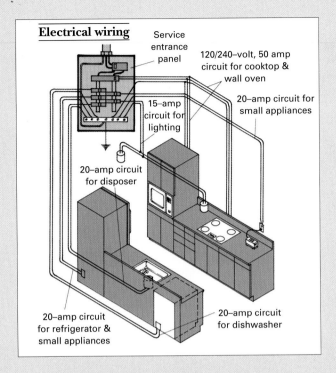

Electrical wiring

- Service entrance panel
- 120/240–volt, 50 amp circuit for cooktop & wall oven
- 15–amp circuit for lighting
- 20–amp circuit for small appliances
- 20–amp circuit for disposer
- 20–amp circuit for refrigerator & small appliances
- 20–amp circuit for dishwasher

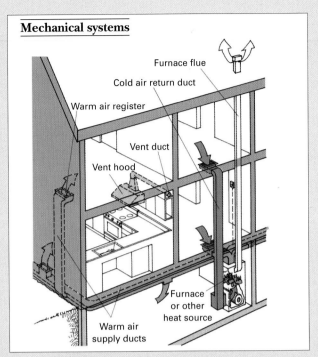

Mechanical systems

- Furnace flue
- Cold air return duct
- Warm air register
- Vent duct
- Vent hood
- Furnace or other heat source
- Warm air supply ducts

ELECTRICAL REQUIREMENTS

Electrical capacity is probably the number one oversight of most homeowners aiming to remodel. New appliances take a lot of power. You may also need new wiring for telephone and other communication media.

- Requirements for electrical circuits are clearly prescribed by the National Electrical Code (NEC). Any outlets near a water source must be protected by ground fault circuit interrupters that cut off power immediately if the current begins leaking anywhere along the circuit.
- Kitchen appliances and whirlpool tubs have specific power requirements; consult the owner's manual or your electrician.
- Older homes with two-wire (120 volts only) service of less than 100 amps can't support major improvements. To add appliances you may need to increase your service type and rating, which means updating the service entrance equipment.
- If you are adding a wall, you may be required by code to add an outlet every 12 feet, or one per wall. In addition, codes may strictly dictate position of outlets and switches.

HEATING AND VENTILATION

Air-conditioning, heating, and ventilation systems may all be affected when you remodel or redecorate. Changes will be governed either by your local plumbing regulations or a separate mechanical code.

- Both air-conditioning and heating ducts are relatively easy to reroute, as long as you can gain access from a basement, crawl space, garage wall, or unfinished attic. Radiant-heat pipes or other slab-embedded systems may pose problems; check them out. Registers are usually easy to reposition; the toespace at the base of cabinets is a favorite spot these days for retrofits. (You can also buy hydronic or electric space heaters designed for these areas.) Don't place any cold air returns in the new kitchen.
- Gas heaters must be vented to the outside.
- Ventilation is critical in kitchens and bathrooms. Even if you have natural ventilation, you should consider adding forced ventilation; it is required by code in windowless bathrooms. In a kitchen, a vent hood can add an attractive focal point, and a discreet downdraft system is especially apt for a new kitchen island or peninsula.

WORKING WITH PROFESSIONALS

WHEN A DESIGN, DECORATING, OR REMODELING JOB is beyond your scope, don't hesitate to turn to a professional for assistance. Although there will be fees for their services, if you finish with the room of your dreams, the money will have been well spent.

CHOOSING A PROFESSIONAL

There are many kinds of designers and building tradespeople, each of whom has different, but sometimes overlapping, skills and services to offer. The following list will help you to begin your search.

Architects

For most decorating endeavors, you will have no need for an architect, but if you are planning a renovation or addition, a state-licensed professional with a degree in architecture may be essential. Architects are trained to create designs that are structurally sound, functional, and aesthetically pleasing. They also know construction materials, can negotiate bids from contractors, and can supervise the actual work. In many communities you are required to have an architect or engineer sign the working drawings for a structure.

Interior designers

Even if you're working with an architect, you may wish to call on the services of an interior designer. These experts specialize in the decorating and furnishing of rooms and can offer fresh, innovative ideas and advice. Through their contacts, a homeowner has access to materials and products not available at the retail level.

- Interior designers have established relationships with upholstery and drapery workrooms, cabinet shops, and tile, painting, and wallpapering contractors, and can supervise them.
- Some interior designers can design kitchens, baths, and basic lighting, or can supervise building contractors.
- Many designers belong to the American Society of Interior Designers (ASID), a professional organization.

Kitchen designers, bathroom designers

Designers who specialize in planning one or both of these rooms often are individuals who are well-informed about the latest trends in furnishings and appliances, but they may have neither the aesthetic skill of a good interior designer nor the structural knowledge of an architect.

- Look for a member of the National Kitchen & Bath Association (NKBA), a Certified Kitchen Designer (CKD), or Certified Bathroom Designer (CBD). Each association has a code of ethics and a continuing program to inform members about the latest techniques and building materials.
- Some cabinet showrooms employ certified designers.

Office designers

Though office designers in the past were engaged to plan large commercial spaces, a new breed specializes in home offices. Like interior designers, office designers understand and have access to the latest materials and products.

Lighting designers

As home design becomes more sophisticated—and room usage more purposeful, professionals become more specialized. Lighting designers specify fixtures and placement of lighting, and they work with a contractor or installer to make a lighting scheme a reality. Their services are particularly helpful for kitchen or office design.

Media center specialists

Cabinetmakers, architects, and interior designers are your best resources for designing custom media centers and wall systems. Remember, however, that planning effective housing of audio and video gear is a specialized art. Be sure the designer you select has experience working with electronics or will consult with the appropriate experts.

- Some electronics retailers have qualified professionals who can work with you and your designer on both planning and installation of media systems.

General contractors

Contractors specialize in construction, although some also have design skills and experience as well. General contractors may do all the work themselves, or they may assume responsibility for hiring qualified subcontractors. They order construction materials and see that the job is completed according to contract. Contractors can also secure building permits and arrange for inspections as work progresses.

• If you ask your contractor to design as well as build, expect to pay for the service.

Subcontractors

If you act as your own general contractor, you will have to hire, coordinate, and supervise subcontractors for specialized jobs such as wiring, plumbing, or tiling. You'll be responsible for permits, insurance, and payroll taxes, as well as direct supervision of all the aspects of construction. Do you have the time or knowledge required for the job? Be sure to assess your energy level carefully!

• Some building codes require that certain kinds of electrical and plumbing work be handled by licensed contractors. Be sure to check, and hire appropriately.

Custom woodcrafters

There are various tradespeople, including cabinetmakers, furniture makers, and finish carpenters, who build shelves and cabinetry. Though there is some overlap, each of these trades is slightly different. To find these people, look in the Yellow Pages under "Cabinetmakers," "Carpenters," "Furniture—Custom Made," "Kitchen Cabinets," and "Woodworkers."

• Nearly all cabinetmakers, whether they're dealers selling manufactured products or local custom woodshops, focus on kitchens and bathrooms. They typically install the units.

• Custom furniture makers work in their own shops and typically handle difficult—and often expensive—projects.

• Finish carpenters are hired by contractors or homeowners to install trim and cabinetry. Their talents range from stapling moldings in place to fine cabinetmaking. Most finish carpenters don't have workshops, so the work is typically done on-site, ruling out complex cabinetmaking (though they do install factory-made cabinets).

Other specialists

Showroom personnel, furniture-store salespeople, building-center staff, and other retailers can sometimes help create the room that's right for you. In fact, this kind of help may be all you need if your requirements are minor. Though some salespeople are quite capable, some may simply be there to sell you more goods.

HIRING A PROFESSIONAL

Whether selecting a designer, a cabinetmaker, or a contractor, start by getting referrals from people you know who have had similar work done. Or you can turn to the Yellow Pages for help. Then call several candidates.

• On the telephone, first ask whether each handles the type of job that you want done and can work within the constraints of your schedule. If so, arrange meetings and ask them to be prepared with references and photos of previous jobs. You may want to visit former clients to check their work firsthand.

• For each type of specialist you wish to hire, obtain several bids for comparison. If you are hiring an architect or designer, discuss your wishes thoroughly; they will explain how their fees are established. When hiring a contractor, provide either an exact description and your own sketches of the desired remodeling, or plans and specifications prepared by an architect or designer. Discuss which aspects of the work the contractor will handle.

• Ask each candidate for a firm bid, based on exactly the same plans or discussions. Have your plans—or intentions—as complete as you can. You don't have to accept the lowest bid; it's more important to choose a reliable, responsible person whose work you admire, and with whom you feel comfortable.

• For some jobs, you may want a written contract, which binds and protects both you and the person you hire. Not just a legal document, a contract is also a list of the expectations of both parties. When every detail is written down, a contract can help minimize the possibility of misunderstandings later. Look it over carefully before signing.

• The contract should clearly identify the participants and define all work to be done, including (as applicable) specific descriptions of all the materials that will be used in the project, the time schedule, and the payment schedule. For a contractor, it should include a set of working drawings. It also should state who is responsible for obtaining permits, and researching whether plans are according to code. Copies of, or affidavits attesting to, subcontractors' licenses and insurance coverage should be included.

PHOTOGRAPHY ACKNOWLEDGMENTS

PHOTOGRAPHERS
Unless noted, all photographs are by *Philip Harvey*.
Andersen Windows: 51 right, 65. *Glenn Christiansen*: 77 bottom right, 235 center. *Crandall & Crandall*: 148 bottom right and left. *Christina del Villar*: 234 left. *David Duncan Livingston*: 6–7, 18, 156. *Steve Marley*: 218. *Marvin Windows & Doors*: 57 top. *Jack McDowell*: 137 center. *Pella® Windows and Doors*: 67 bottom. *Norman Plate*: 37 bottom, 118, 155 top right, 180 bottom left and right, 183 top right, 235 left, 246, 260 bottom right, 267 top. *Chad Slattery*: 257 top right. *Darrow M. Watt*: 136 left. *Alan Weintraub*: 251 right. *Russ Widstrand*: 235 right. *Tom Wyatt*: 13, 19, 31 right, 72 top, 91 bottom right, 127 bottom, 130 left, 131, 136 right, 157 left, 219 right, 220 bottom left and right, 221, 222, 223, 226, 227, 228 top right, bottom, 229 top right, bottom left and right, 230, 231, 233 top, 234 center, right, 236 center, bottom, 238, 239, 242, bottom left.

DESIGNERS
Unless noted, all credits are for interior or architectural design.
Part 1
6–7: David Duncan Livingston. 8: Interior: John Schneider, ASID. Architecture: David Martin, AIA. Lighting: Linda Ferry. 9 *right:* Decorative Painting: Claire Roman. 10: Cheryl Driver of Hilary Thatz, Inc. Decorative Painting: David Mattice of Evans & Brown. 11: Epifanio Juarez/Juarez Design. Interior Architecture and Design: Scott Design. 12: Myrna Baldwin, Baldwin Interiors. Window Treatment: Linda Deskins. 13: MacKenzie C. Patterson. 14: Jan Higgins. Window Treatment: Hana Shoji & Interiors. 15 *top:* Osburn Design. 15 *bottom:* Architectural Kitchens & Baths. 16: J. Reed Robbins. 17 *top:* Abigail Crocker Design. Decorative Painting: Samantha Renko Design. Fabric Treatments: Merryl Latini. 17 *bottom:* Betty Lou Phillips, ASID. 18: David Duncan Livingston. 19 *top:* Thomas Bartlett Interiors of Napa. 19 *bottom:* Osburn Design. Decorative Painting: Iris Potter. 20: Epifanio Juarez/Juarez Design. Interior Architecture and Design: Scott Design. 21: Schweitzer Bim/Josh Schweitzer. 22 *top:* James Gillam Architects. Interior: Jane Nissen Laidley. 22 *bottom:* Churchill & Hambelton Architects.

PART 2
24–25: Barbara Scavullo Design. 26–27: Thomas Bartlett Interiors. 28: Sharon Legallet and Bebe Trinker, ISID, Legallet-Trinker Associates. 29: Design and Decorative Painting: Peggy Del Rosario. 30 *bottom:* David Stonesifer of Los Gatos Porch. Decorative Painting: Claire Roman. 31 *right:* Julie Atwood Design. 30 *top:* Ralph E. A. Frischman, Myra Posert Design Co., and Jan Tetzlaff/Arabesque. 34: Daniel W. Winey/Cheri Varnum. 35 *top:* Courtyard Collection. 35 *bottom:* Thomas Bartlett

Interiors. 36: Bauer Interior Design. 37 *top:* Osburn Design. 37 *bottom:* William & Dutcher. 40 *left:* Warren Sheets Design. 40 *right:* Barbara Scavullo Design. 41: Remick Associates. 42: Hendrix/Alardyce. 43 *top:* Kuth/Ranieri. Melinda Morrison Lighting Design. 43 *bottom:* Architecture: House + House of San Francisco. Interior: Osburn Design. 44 *top left:* Mary T. Rice, Decorating Den. Window Treatment: Bill Dahl, Bestline. 44 *top right:* Window Treatment: Rossetti & Corriea. 44 *bottom:* Interior and Lighting: Kenton Knapp, ASID, CID. 45: Osburn Design. 46 *top left:* Michelle Raimondi of Raimondi's Paint & Wallpaper and Stephen M. Boyce. 46 *top right:* Sandra Keating of Nesting Instincts. 46 *bottom left:* Bradbury & Bradbury Art Wallpapers. 46 *bottom right:* Upholstered Walls: Tony Vella. 47: Heidi Emmett. 48–49: Morimoto Architects. 50: Ruth Soforenko, ASID. 51 *left:* House + House of San Francisco. 51 *right:* Andersen Windows. 52 *top left:* Raymond L. Lloyd. Glazing: Alan Masaoka Architectural Glass. 52 *top right:* Churchill & Hambelton Architects. 52 *bottom:* Charles Debbas. 53 *top left:* Glazing: Alan Masaoka Architectural Glass. 53 *top center:* Remick Associates. 53 *top right:* Remick Associates. Glazing: Alan Masaoka Architectural Glass. 53 *bottom:* Remick Associates. 54 *top:* MRD Design. 54–55: Nan Rosenblatt. 55 *top right:* Fisher-Friedman Associates. 56 *top:* Window Treatment: Muffy Hook. 56 *bottom left:* Barbara Mack, Fleece to Fibers Interior Design. 56 *bottom center:* Morimoto Architects. Glazing: Alan Masaoka Architectural Glass. 56 *bottom right:* Architecture: House + House of San Francisco. Interior: Osburn Design. 57 *bottom:* Window Treatment: Muffy Hook. 58 *top:* Backen Arragoni & Ross. 59 *right:* Osburn Design. 58–59: Churchill & Hambelton Architects. 60 *top left:* Morimoto Architects. 60 *top right:* Bredthauer/Curran & Associates. 61 *top:* Marily Riding Design. 61 *bottom:* Lequita Vance-Watkins/adVance Design of Carmel. 62: Bredthauer/Curran & Associates. 63 *left:* Rick Sambol/Kitchen Consultants. 63 *right:* Raymond L. Lloyd. 66: House + House of San Francisco. 67 *top:* George Brook-Kothlow & Associates. 67 *bottom:* Pella/Rolscreen. 68–69: David Turner and John Martin/Turner Martin. 70: Window Treatment: Muffy Hook. Decorative Painting: Michelle Marta-Drake. 72 *top:* Fontenot Designs. 72 *bottom:* Decorative Painting: Shelley Masters Studio. 73: House + House of San Francisco. 76 *top:* Interior Design and Decorative Painting: Peggy Del Rosario. 76 *bottom:* Sanborn Design, Inc. and Courtyard Collections. 77 *top:* Ann Jones, Interiors. Decorative Painting: Adele Crawford, Painted Finishes. 77 *bottom left:* Charleen Matoza of La Fille du roi Antiques & Interiors. Decorative Painting: Tina Martinez of Furniture Art Studio. 77 *bottom right:* Robert W. Miller. 78: Jeanese Rowell Interiors. Decorative Painting: Karen Sickel. 79 *top:* Barbara McDowell. 79 *bottom:* Pierre Deux Original Fabrics. 80 *top:* Mona Branagh of Pacific Interiors. 80 *bottom:* Carlene Anderson of Kitchen Design Inc. 81: Catherine Campbell Interiors. 85 *center:*

Janice M. Stein of Villa Associates. Upholstered Walls: Douglas Griggs of Hang Ups. 85 *bottom:* Interior and Lighting: Kenton Knapp, ASID, CID. 86 *left:* Pierre Deux Original Fabrics. 86 *right:* Tedrick & Bennett. Upholstered Walls: Douglas Gripps of Hang Ups. 87: Georgia Johnstone Designs, Inc. 90 *top left:* Olson/Sundberg Architects. 90 *top right:* Lighting: Linda Ferry. Interior: Michelle Pheasant Design. Architecture: Charles Rose. 90 *bottom:* Buff, Smith & Hensman, Architects. Interior: Bob Moore. 91 *top right:* Ace Architects. 91 *left, bottom right:* Osburn Design. 92 *right:* Suzanne Tucker McMicking. Restoration: Steve Anderson of Wood Think It Was New. 92: Remick Associates. 93 *bottom:* John Tobler. 93 *top:* Remick Associates. 94: Restoration: Steve Anderson of Wood Think It Was New. 95: Sherry Faure of Faure Design and Lila Levinson of Accent on Design. 98–99: Peggy Del Rosario. 100–101: Corinne Wiley, ASID. 102 *left:* Thomas Bartlett Interiors of Napa. 102 *right:* Kelly Heim. 103: Dianna Coppersmith Interiors of Marin. 104: Charleen Matoza, La Fille Du Roi Interiors. Window Treatment: C. C. Cahoots Custom Sewing. 105 *top:* Tedrick & Bennett Associates. 105 *bottom:* Orchard's Lazy K House. Window Treatment: Muffy Hook. 106: Lindstrom Co. Window Treatment: J C Penny Custom Decorating. 107: Janet Dutka Interior Architect & Design. 108: Shelby De Quesada of Shelby Co. 110 *top left:* Window Treatment: Muffy Hook. 110 *top right:* Cheryl Driver of Hilary Thatz, Inc. Decorative Painting: David Mattice of Evans & Brown. 110 *bottom:* Sharon Legallet and Bebe Trinker, ISID, Legallet-Trinker Associates. 111 *bottom left:* Charleen Matoza, La Fille Du Roi Interiors. Window Treatment: C. C. Cahoots Custom Sewing. 111 *top:* Pat Davis Interiors Window Treatment: Diana Jones. 111 *bottom right:* Betty Lou Phillips, ASID. 112: Ruth Soforenko Associates. Joseph Bellomo. 113: Fehrman Interior Design Inc. Window Treatment: Opulence Ltd. 114: Julie Atwood Design & Restoration. Window Treatment: Lun-On Company. 116 *left:* Cynthia Brian of Starstyle Interiors. 116 *right:* Brian Peters. 117: Ruth Soforenko Associates. Heidi Hanson, AIA. 119 *top:* Julie Atwood Design & Restoration. Window Treatment: Lun-On Company. 119 *bottom:* Sharon Campbell, ASID. Fabric Painting: Victoria Bohlman. 120: Edgar R. Dethlefsen. Window Treatment: Hana Shoji & Interiors. 121 *top:* Julie Atwood Design & Restoration. Window Treatment: Roger Arlington Fabrics. 122: Jacobson, Silverstein & Winslow Architects/Paul Winans Construction, Inc. 123 *right:* Amoroso/Holman Design Group. 124–125: Agnes Bourne, Inc. 125: Morimoto Architects. 126: Laura Taylor Moore, Interior Services of Los Gatos/Betty Benesi, Cottage Industries. 127 *top:* Dave Terpening/Churchill & Hambelton Architects. 127 *bottom:* Osburn Design. 128: Architecture: Robert H. Waterman/Waterman & Sun. Interior: Robert W. Miller, ASID/Flegel's. 129 *bottom:* Osburn Design. 129 *top:* Jim Olson/Olson Sundberg Architects. 130 *right:* Lighting: Randall Whitehead/Light Source. 130 *left:* Suzan

Nettleship. General Contractor: Iris Harrell. **131:** Rushton/Chartock. **132:** Lighting: Carol DePelecyn, Christopher Thompson. Interior: Carollyne Coby, Design 5 International. Architects: GGLO/Bill Gaylord and William Castillo. **133 top:** Sharon Sistine. **133 bottom:** Legallet-Trinker Design Associates. Upholstery: Douglas Griggs/Hang Ups. **134:** Osburn Design. **135 bottom:** The Schutte Hayes Group. **137 right:** Osburn Design.

PART 3
138–139: Lee Von Hasseln. Lighting: Linda Ferry. **140:** Carrasco & Associates. **142:** Jim Olson/Olson Sundberg Architects. **143:** Buff, Smith & Hensman, Architects. Interior: Bob Moore. **144 bottom:** Interior Design and Decorative Painting: Peggy Del Rosario. **144 top:** Van-Martin Rowe Interior Design Studio. **145:** Kotas-Pantaleoni Architects. **146 top:** Jon Sather Erlandson. **146 bottom:** Lawrence Masnada. Lighting: Randall Whitehead/Light Source. **148 top right and left:** Steven Stein/Miller-Stein. **148 bottom right and left:** Calvin L. Smith Associates, Inc. **149 top right and left:** Sanborn Designs Incorporated. **149 bottom:** Remick Associates. **150:** Remick Associates. **151:** Robert W. Miller, ASID, Flegel's Home Furnishings. **152 top:** Barbara Jacobs and Janice Naymark of Barbara Jacobs Interior Design. Lighting: Randall Whitehead/Light Source. Pendant Fixture Design and Fabrication: Pam Morris/Exciting Lighting. **152 bottom:** George Suyama Architects. **153 top:** Kuth/Ranieri. Lighting: Melinda Morrison Lighting Design. **153 bottom:** Mike Moore for Mike Furniture. **154 bottom:** Amoroso/Holman Design Group. **154 top:** Gary Earl Parsons. **155 top left:** Mui Ho. **155 bottom right:** Bauer Interior Design. **155 top right:** Richard Watson. **155 bottom left:** Amoroso/Holman Design Group. **156:** Sharon Campbell, ASID. **157 right:** Design: Epifanio Juarez/Juarez Design. Interior Architecture and Design: Scott Design. **157 left:** Suzan Nettleship. General Contractor: Iris Harrell. **158 top:** Window Treatment: Muffy Hook. **158 bottom:** Carol S. Shawn. **159:** Olson Sundberg Architects. **160 top left:** Teresa Quigley of Spending Wives Design. **160 bottom:** Lorin Nelson & Mackin Conservatories. **160 top right:** Churchill & Hambelton Architects. **161:** Charles Debbas. **162 left:** Van-Martin Rowe Interior Design Studio. **162 right:** Cody Associates. **163 top left:** Nicole Patton Interiors. **163 top right:** Architecture: Luther M. Hintz, AIA. Interior: Pamela Pearce Design. **163 bottom:** Karen Davis and Canada College Student ASID. Window Treatment: Marti M. Woo. **164 right:** Ralph Frischman/Design & Decoration and Carol Romano/Romano Design. **164 left, 165 top right:** Brian A. Murphy and Fro Vakili/BAM Construction/Design. **165 top left:** Backen Arragoni & Ross. **165 top right:** Lee Von Hasseln. Lighting: Linda Ferry. **165 bottom left:** Kuth/Ranieri. Lighting: Melinda Morrison LightingDesign. **166:** Mui Ho. **168:** Erika Brunson Design Associates. **169:** Brian Brand/Baylis Brand Wagner Architects. Interior: R.W. Burton Designs. **170: top:** Ruth Livingston. **170 bottom:** Robert Scott

Cates/N.L. Tobiason Interior Design. **171:** Techline Studios. **172:** Osburn Design. **173:** Sharon Campell, ASID. **174 bottom:** Marc Melvin/Agnes Bourne, Inc. **176:** Sanborn Designs Incorporated. **177 top:** James E. Bolen Interior Planning & Design. **177 bottom:** J. Allen Sayles. **180 top left:** Helen L. Carreker, ASID. **180 bottom left and right:** Terry Anne Meckler and James Vogler. **180 top right:** Van-Martin Rowe Interior Design Studio. **181:** Jan Fillinger/Savidge Warren Architects. **182:** Fernau & Hartman Architects. **183 top right:** Boyd/Jenks Associates. **183 top right and bottom:** Rockwood Design & Judith Marshall. **184 top:** Samson McCann. **184 bottom:** Decorative Painting: Ann Blair Davidson. **185:** Sanborn Designs Incorporated. **186 left:** Sharon M. Campbell. Decorative Painting: Susan Eslick. **186 right:** Sally Sirkin Lewis Interior Design. Custom Furniture: Sally Sirkin Lewis/J. Robert Scott & Associates, Inc. **188–189:** Gary Hutton Design. **190:** Marc Melvin/Agnes Bourne, Inc. **191 top right:** Ruth Livingston. **191 bottom left:** Osburn Design. **191 top right:** Sharon Campell, ASID. **191 bottom right:** Janet Lohman Interior Design. **192:** Courtyard Collections. **194:** Remick Associates. **195, 196:** Thomas Bartlett Interiors. **197:** Mark Chastain and Susan Lind Chastain of Fine Custom Sewing. Decorative Painting: Spike Lind (ribbons), Barry Nelson and Bill Sandoval (background). **198:** Betty Lou Phillips, ASID. **200 top:** Fontenot Designs. **200 bottom right:** Ellen Alvarez/Design Cabinet Showrooms. **200 bottom left:** Architectural Kitchens & Baths. **201 top:** Betty Lou Phillips, ASID. **201 bottom right:** Stephen W. Sanborn. **201 bottom left:** Marilyn Riding Design. **202 center left:** Nicole Patton Interiors. **203 top right:** J. Reed Robbins. **202–203:** Design: J. Reed Robbins. Antique Accessories: Lottie Ballou Classic Clothing. **204:** Jacobson, Silverstein & Winslow Architects/Paul Winans Construction, Inc. **205:** J. Reed Robbins. **206 top:** Morimoto Architects. **206 bottom:** Architectural Kitchens & Baths. **207:** Oz Designs/Linda Osborn. **208:** Ralph E. A. Frischman, Myra Posert Design Co., and Jan Tezlaff/Arabesque. **210 top:** Nancy Rubenstein and Jeanne White Interiors. **210 bottom:** Window Treatment: Rosetti & Corriea Draperies, Inc. **211:** Alexander & Byrd, Interior Design Associates. **212 top:** David Rivera Designs, Inc. **212 bottom:** Chet Setterlund. **215 bottom:** Croworks and Joyce Bohlman Designs. **215 top:** Juvenile Lifestyles, Inc. **216 top:** Kuth/Ranieri. Lighting: Melinda Morrison Lighting Design. **216 bottom:** Ann Maurice Interior Design. Lighting: Terry Ohm. **217 top right:** Lee Von Hasseln. Lighting: Linda Ferry. **217 bottom right:** House + House of San Francisco. **217 bottom left:** Remick Associates. **217 top left:** Lee Von Hasseln. Lighting: Linda Ferry. **218:** Remick Associates. **220 bottom left and right:** J. Allen Sayles/Architectural Kitchens & Baths. **221:** Rob Wellington Quigley. **222 center:** William Turnbull. **222 top, 223 top:** Wally Brueske/Design Cabinet Showrooms. **223 bottom:** Kirby Fitzpatrick. **224:** Sheila Einhorn Interior Design and Unlimited Fricke. **226:** Adele Crawford Painted Finishes. **227 top and**

bottom: Osburn Design. **228 top left:** Terry Sanders, Virginia Smith, Sharry Hicky, and Georganne Thurston. Sconce Mosaic: Karen Thompson/Archetile. **228 bottom:** Shakespeare & Burns. **228 top right:** Remick Associates. **229 top left:** Carlene Anderson Kitchen Design, Inc. **229 top right:** Jerri Golden. **229 bottom left:** Suzan Nettleship. General Contractor: Iris Harrell. **229 bottom right:** Wally Brueske/Design Cabinet Showrooms. **230:** Plus Kitchen. **231 top:** Osburn Design/Lepelley Custom Cabinets. **231 bottom:** Osburn Design. **232 top:** Carlene Anderson Kitchen Design, Inc. **232 bottom:** Nan Rosenblatt. **233 bottom:** John Newcomb. Lighting: Linda Ferry. **233 top:** Plus Kitchens. **236 center and bottom:** J. Allen Sayles/Architectural Kitchens & Baths. **237:** Churchill & Hambelton Architects. **238:** Thomas Bartlett Interiors of Napa. **239:** Remick Associates. **242 top left:** Carrasco & Associates Architects. Interior and Lighting: Margaret M. Wimmer. **242 top right:** Epifanio Juarez/Juarez Design. Interior Architecture and Design: Scott Design. **242 bottom left:** Wally Brueske/Design Cabinet Showrooms. **242 bottom right:** Sheila Einhorn Interior Design and Unlimited Fricke. **243:** Kuth/Ranieri. Lighting: Melinda Morrison Lighting Design. **244:** Raymond L. Lloyd. Interior: Michael Assum/Mark Twisselman. **246:** Kurt B. Anderson/Andarch Associates. **247:** Pulte Home Corporation. **248 top:** Laurence Allen. **248 bottom:** Kuth/Ranieri. Lighting: Melinda Morrison Lighting Design. **249:** Ted T. Tanaka. **251 left:** J. Allen Sayles. Interior: Charlotte Boyle Interiors. **251 right:** Carson Bowler/Bowler & Cook Architects. Interior: Rainier Concepts Ltd. **252–253:** Remick Associates. **256 top:** Paul Vincent Wiseman. **256 bottom:** House + House of San Francisco. **257 top left:** Gerald N. Jacobs/Jacobs Design. **257 top right:** Diane Stevenson Design. Glazing: Alan Masaoka Archtectural Glass. **257 bottom left:** Morimoto Architects. **257 bottom right:** Raymond L. Lloyd. Interior: Michael Assum/Mark Twisselman. **258:** Jack Buktenica Associates. Interior: Courtyard Collection. **259:** Backen Arragoni & Ross. **260 top:** Patrick Sheridan. **260 bottom right:** Molly Ruth Hale. **260 bottom left:** Osburn Design. **261 top left:** Decorative Painting: The Beardsley Company. **261 top right:** Remick Associates. **261 bottom left:** Raymond L. Lloyd. Interior: Michael Assum/Mark Twisselman. **261 bottom right:** Ted T. Tanaka. **262–263:** Lequita Vance-Watkins/adVance Design of Carmel. **264:** Remick Associates. **265:** Osburn Design. **266 top left:** Rick Sambol/Kitchen Consultants and Lynne Shilling. **266 top right:** Obie Bowman. **266 bottom left:** Debra Gutierrez. **266 bottom right:** House + House of San Francisco. **267 top:** Richard Elmore. **267 bottom:** Rick Sambol/Kitchen Consultants. **268 top:** Backen Arragoni & Ross. **268 bottom:** Osburn Design. **269 top left:** Remick Associates. **269 bottom:** Kuth/Ranieri. Lighting: Melinda Morrison Lighting Design.

PART 4
279–280: Backen Arragoni & Ross.

Index